Autism in the secondary classroom

Strategies and resources to support successful inclusion

By **Joy Beaney** and **Penny Kershaw**

With illustrations by **Haitham Al-Ghani**

First edition first published 2006 by The National Autistic Society
393 City Road, London EC1V 1NG
www.autism.org.uk

New edition first published 2014

ISBN 978 1 905722 68 6

Written by **Joy Beaney** and **Penny Kershaw**

Illustrations by **Haitham Al-Ghani**

Edited by **Rodgers & Johns Publications** and **Eleanor Wheeler**

Designed by **Claire Lythgoe**

Printed by **RAP Spiderweb Ltd**

Contents

About the authors and illustrator

Joy Beaney, MA, has many years' experience working with children with autism in mainstream and special education. She has been in charge of a facility for children with autism that was attached to a mainstream primary school, an assistant head at a special school and the manager of an inclusion support service that provided training and outreach support for staff in mainstream schools. She has completed research for the National College of Teaching and Leadership on the key features of a successful inclusion support service. Joy has always had a passion for breaking down barriers to learning and enabling children to fulfil their full potential and this has been further developed through her research into the impact of sensory difficulties in children with autism. She has published a sensory assessment and intervention programme and is a member of the Autism Education Trust's Expert Reference Group.

Joy promotes and shares best practice through delivering training on aspects of autism nationally and internationally on different types of courses.

Children with autism have very special needs. Joy's determination to understand and help these children achieve their full potential, no matter what their ability, led her to develop these ideas into this book.

Penny Kershaw, MEd, NPQH, is a school leader and autism professional. She currently works in primary and secondary special schools. She has been involved in international research projects, leading mainstream outreach services and working as a special educational needs co-ordinator in an inner London primary school. Penny delivers a variety of successful continuing professional development (CPD) courses for various professionals, family members and charities.

Penny's research and practice focuses on developing an insight into how people with autism learn and interpret the world around them. She has published widely on understanding the autism diagnosis, strategies to support students with autism in schools, and CPD for school staff.

Penny has extensive knowledge of advising school staff and teaching children with autism spectrum disorders in various settings. She was inspired to write this book after working alongside many teachers in mainstream schools whose pupils had benefited from her practical ideas and specialist experience.

Joy and Penny have collaborated on two research scholarships for the Department of Education entitled *Developing the Thinking Skills of Children with Autism* and *Using Visual Support*. They have also published another book for The National Autistic Society, *Inclusion in the Primary Classroom*, and have written articles for special educational needs (SEN) journals.

Haitham Al-Ghani, who has autism, is an author, cartoon animator and illustrator of children's books. Author of *The Red Beast*, he has a triple distinction in Multimedia Studies and was the 2007 winner of the Vincent Lines Award for creative excellence.

Author acknowledgements

Thank you for the commitment that staff at the schools where we work have given us while we have been developing our ideas. Their feedback has helped us to refine and implement strategies.

We would like to thank **Haitham Al-Ghani** for allowing us to print his symbols and artwork. We would also like to acknowledge the support parents have given us. We have found the insights they have shared about their children to have been invaluable.

Foreword

As a result of our work supporting staff and students in mainstream schools, we have devised strategies to promote successful inclusion.

The learning support department in any secondary school is the first port of call for students with autism and their parents. The strategies explained in this book will be an invaluable resource for SENCOs and teaching assistants working in this department. Providing this support is crucial in a large school setting.

School is a social environment and students with autism often find the social expectations of others difficult to cope with.

By being aware of potential problems for students it is hoped that those in the learning support department can help them avoid difficulties during the school day.

Raising the awareness of subject teachers will help them to use a variety of teaching strategies suitable for students with autism.

Throughout our book we have used the terms autism, autism spectrum disorder and ASD interchangeably.

1. Autism

The National Autistic Society defines autism as:

> **a lifelong developmental disability that affects how a person communicates with, and relates to, other people. It also affects how they make sense of the world around them.**
> NAS website (2014)

The condition was described by **Leo Kanner** in 1943. He believed that autism resulted from problems occurring in the developing brain. Initially many parents do not notice that their child is not developing in the same way as other children. But at around the age of two to three, when there is generally a great improvement in social skills and communication, a child with autism's developmental differences become more obvious.

All pupils are different and the way autism affects individuals is very variable, so the term autism spectrum disorder or ASD is often used. Some people do not consider autism to be a disorder and think of it in terms of having a different style of thinking. They prefer to call it an autism spectrum condition or ASC.

Features of autism

To have a diagnosis of an autism spectrum disorder a person must have certain features.

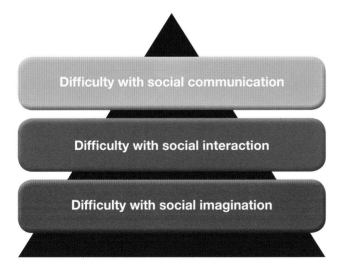

These features are often referred to as 'the triad of impairments'. The individual must have difficulties in all three areas for a diagnosis of autism to be made.

Lorna Wing, an expert on autism, believes that autism includes a spectrum of disorders, which form a continuum.

Mild difficulty	Moderate difficulty	Severe difficulty
Difficulty with social interaction		
› can initiate interaction › has difficulty coping in group situations › lacks empathy	› tolerates some interaction but does not seek social contact	› not interested in social contact
Difficulty with social communication		
› talks about subjects based around their own interests › does not take account of the listener and often continues to talk when others are not interested	› attempts to communicate basic needs	› feels no need to communicate with others
Difficulty with social imagination		
› lacks understanding of subtle social rules › has difficulty understanding that other people have different views or thoughts from themselves › lacks spontaneity › seeks explanation of different or new situations	› actions or speech may be very repetitive › resists unfamiliar or new ideas if not adequately prepared › has difficulty generalising learning	› lack of imagination › cannot anticipate the future › lacks strategies to cope with change or new circumstances, however minor

Chapter 1: Autism

Strengths and differences

Some people with autism may exhibit other features. These more unusual aspects of thought and behaviour could cause major problems for pupils in the mainstream classroom. However, some of the features can also be strengths, and understanding them will help staff to address them when teaching pupils with autism, so they can reach their full potential. These features are discussed below.

Visual skills

Some people with autism say they think in pictures and many have good visual memories. Using a visual approach in the classroom is vital to enable pupils to get the most from a lesson.

An excellent rote memory

Encouraging rote learning can be a useful approach for teachers to use in some subject areas, though they need to be aware that a pupil's expertise at reciting information can mask their lack of understanding of a topic.

Organisational skills

Pupils with autism find it hard to organise themselves but can follow existing routines. Once routines and work schedules are set up pupils with autism can easily follow them and such routines can give them confidence and reduce stress. Problems with organisation and planning are some of the difficulties referred to as executive dysfunction (see Chapter 4, page 18).

Restricted or obsessive interests

A pupil's interests can become 'all consuming'. For example, pupils may become so obsessed with an interest such as trains that they have difficulty focusing on anything else. It is always best to incorporate pupils' interests into work if possible. Trying to get rid of an obsession is not usually recommended as another will probably replace it, which could be even worse! Pupils may be highly knowledgeable about their interests and spend a long time finding out about the subject.

Obsessive desire for sameness

Pupils may have an overwhelming need to organise according to their own criteria, for example, enter a room and arrange all the items on the teacher's desk so that it is tidy! Children with autism prefer familiarity: a young child will probably go towards and explore a new toy, but a child with autism will probably avoid the new one in favour of a familiar one. New experiences or changes to routine can be threatening for pupils with autism as this creates uncertainty and leads to great anxiety.

Preoccupation and processing parts of objects rather than the whole

This is sometimes referred to as central coherence deficit. Children with autism may spend too much time concentrating on one small part of an object or task and have difficulty connecting concepts. For example, they might play with the wheels on a toy car rather than the car itself. Pupils with autism need help to see the whole picture or overview.

Wendy Lawson, an adult with autism, explained her difficulties with generalising information as follows:

> **We tend not to take what we have learnt from one situation and apply it to another. This means that every situation is seen as new and this has major implications for the children's ability to generalise their learning.**
> Lawson (2000, p38)

Sensory difficulties

If the brain does not process information from our senses effectively, and does not organise the information coming into the brain, pupils may display unusual reactions to sensory stimuli. There are many ways in which sensory systems may dysfunction. Many individuals with autism may be overly sensitive to certain sensations (be hypersensitive), as a result of too much stimulation reaching the brain, or have low sensitivity (be hyposensitive) where too little stimulation reaches the brain.

Sensory difficulties can affect any of the senses. For example, hypersensitivity can result in touch being painful so that pupils may react violently if someone brushes past and gently touches them. A pupil may cover their ears to block out sound and scream in response to the sound of a hand dryer if they are hypersensitive to sound. Smells can be intensified and become overpowering. Pupils may have difficulty tolerating movement and they may be frightened of activities where their feet leave the ground.

All these examples of sensory difficulties can easily lead to sensory overload. This can cause different reactions and behaviours that challenge: pupils may 'shut down' and try to block out the stimulus, try to escape from the situation, or become verbally or physically aggressive.

Longhorn described the difficulty some children have in processing sensory information:

> **The sensory information that may get through to the brain has become fragmented, meaningless, unpredictable and often very scary. So the child sets up barriers, withdraws, has tantrums and then escapes into his/her carefully selected (and to them, safe) sensory world.**
> Longhorn (in Powell, 2000, p30)

If a pupil is upset we are apt to increase stimulation by approaching them or talking to them. This can increase anxiety in pupils with autism. For a variety of reasons, anxiety can build up during the day and then pupils 'blow'. It is therefore very important to find out what the trigger is that caused a behaviour issue and try to avoid it.

Unusual fears or phobias

Pupils may be very frightened of objects or situations which do not appear threatening to others. It is important for people working with pupils with autism to be understanding and recognise their fears. For example, these pupils may refuse to enter the toilets in case the hand dryer makes a noise. Many of these fears could be related to their sensory difficulties.

Repetitive body movements

A pupil with autism may exhibit unusual behaviour such as flapping their hands or rocking back and forth. This could be a calming exercise for them, but might draw a teacher's attention from others in the class. Wilkes believes that these repetitive behaviours are often a direct reaction to a sensory experience:

> **It is therefore understandable why individuals with autism create rituals or self-stimulatory behaviours such as spinning, flapping, tapping because these make them feel that they are in control and feel safe in their unique world.**
> Wilkes (2005, p3)

Repetitive or inappropriate speech

Pupils with autism may repeat phrases or continue to talk about their particular interest unaware that others are not interested, or that the subject is considered inappropriate.

Overly formal speech

It is important to be aware that pupils with autism may speak in a highly formal or detailed manner. Their apparent high level of expressive language can hide a lack of understanding of a topic and lack of ability to recognise social conventions.

Repetitive routines

Pupils may repeat actions, for example they might line up pencils over and over and over again. As a result of this liking of or need for routine and order, pupils with autism are often precise and accurate. They often produce very neat, careful work and enjoy educational activities that are repetitive and which many pupils without autism would find 'boring'.

Problem with joint attention

Pupils may not follow your gaze when you are pointing at an object. You may have problems sharing and engaging attention and once you have got a pupil's attention it may be difficult to disengage.

Chapter 1: Autism

Comprehension

Pupils with autism may be good at word recognition but may not have a good understanding of what they have read. They may need help to find the relevant parts of the text in order to make sense of it, and to grasp subtle meanings or 'subtext'.

Processing language

Pupils with autism may need a lot longer than other pupils to process language and it is important that teachers wait and allow them time to answer questions.

Empathising with others

Pupils with autism may have problems empathising. For example, they often do not realise other people have ideas or thoughts that differ from their own. This can lead to misunderstanding, as pupils do not see the need to explain a situation to a teacher or teaching assistant as they think they already know what has happened. They also may not realise that their remarks could cause embarrassment or offence. This difficulty is often referred to as lack of 'theory of mind'.

Delayed play skills

At approximately two years of age, typically developing children begin to engage in pretend play. They are able to imagine an object is something it is not; for example, a child may pretend a brick is a train. Children with autism take longer developing this stage in play and when they start school their play may still be limited to the physical exploration of objects. As these children get older they often prefer to play with younger children whose play is at their developmental level.

Islets of ability

Pupils with autism often have uneven and erratic cognitive profiles; for example they may excel at science and be very poor in maths. It is essential to make a variety of thorough assessments. If you are assessing and a pupil knows fact 'c' you cannot assume she or he knows fact 'a' and fact 'b'. Pupils with autism have difficulty concentrating. If the input to a lesson is auditory they will probably miss huge chunks of information.

Asperger syndrome and high-functioning autism

Some pupils with autism in primary schools have a diagnosis of Asperger syndrome. Hans Asperger was an Austrian paediatrician who first described the syndrome in 1944, but his work was not translated into English until 1991. Lorna Wing was the first person to use the term Asperger syndrome in a paper published in 1981.

Asperger syndrome is often associated with the more able children on the autism spectrum who are likely to be more verbal and want to socialise. It is generally agreed that children with a diagnosis of autism or Asperger syndrome manifest the same triad of impairments that Lorna Wing described (see table on page 9), and therefore similar intervention techniques are helpful. Pupils who fall into this category are likely to be able to achieve well academically, especially in more formal, less creative subjects such as maths. However, they may still need significant support in social situations, to maintain positive behaviour and to develop organisational skills.

There are particular areas that may cause these pupils to have difficulty 'fitting in' and gaining peer acceptance, which are discussed below.

Making friends

Problems making and sustaining friendships can be a great source of unhappiness and can lead to depression or an increase in aggressive behaviour.

Rigid thinking or inflexibility of thought

Pupils with Asperger syndrome may find it hard to cope with sudden changes and to move from familiar situations to unfamiliar ones. Strategies to help with lesson changeover and other transition times need careful planning. They may have problems coping with the differing behavioural expectations of the different staff they encounter during the day. These pupils often have no tact and may just say what they are thinking! They can often appear rude and staff need to be made aware of this so they can understand, make allowances and give guidance.

Lack of social awareness

Most pupils with Asperger syndrome want friends and would like to join in activities with their peers, but they are likely to have poor social skills and often do not understand their peer group's rules or behaviour. Therefore they can easily become a target for bullying and the school staff need to be aware of the pupils who are particularly at risk. Some pupils may find eye contact difficult, which could result in them being thought of as rude. These pupils are often not aware of other people's personal space and may stand too close, which can make others feel uncomfortable or threatened. They may not pick up meaning from others' body language or realise that someone is getting angry. Some pupils may have interests that can become an obsession, and be unable to understand that others are not interested in the same thing.

Impaired communication skills

Pupils with Asperger syndrome can often have a well-developed vocabulary but still have difficulty communicating with others. They often take things literally and therefore do not understand jokes or sarcasm. They frequently talk about their own interests and do not take the audience into account. Some pupils with Asperger syndrome talk in a loud voice with little intonation.

Poor coordination

Some pupils with Asperger syndrome have poor coordination and exhibit odd mannerisms. This can affect their performance in sport and could result in them being bullied.

> **In autism, effective teaching can only be realised by an initial consideration of the individual's way of learning and its effects on whatever the teacher might plan to do. Education in autism needs to be pursued from the child's perspective.**
> Powell (2000, p148)

Changes to the diagnosis of autism

The criteria for making a diagnosis of autism is periodically reviewed to reflect current research. The main criterion used in the UK is the World Health Organization's International Classification of Diseases (ICD). In 2012 the American Psychiatric Association revised its Diagnostic and Statistical Manual (DSM-5).

These are the DSM-5's criteria for a diagnosis of autism:

1 difficulties with social communication and interaction

2 restricted, repetitive patterns of behaviour, interests or activities

The DSM-5 emphasises the importance of identifying a child's needs and how much their autism affects their ability to function in everyday life. Sensory difficulties are included in the diagnostic criteria for the first time under the section on restricted, repetitive patterns of behaviour, interests or activities. The DSM-5 describes the condition of autism as an autism spectrum disorder and states that individual descriptors such as Asperger syndrome will no longer be used. In the UK there are no immediate plans to change the way a diagnosis of autism or Asperger syndrome is made.

A diagnosis of autism does not reflect anything about intelligence but is an assessment of how much the child exhibits the characteristics of autism. For example, a highly intelligent child could display extremely noticeable autistic behaviour whereas a child with lower intelligence may exhibit much less noticeable autistic behaviour, and vice versa.

2. Developing a person-centred approach

Some students in school require additional help and support. Statements of special education need (SEN) have been replaced with education, health and care (EHC) plans. These plans put the child and family at the centre of the assessment and planning process to make sure their views are understood. This is called person-centred planning and its aim is to focus on the needs and aspirations of the child, increasing choice and control over the plan. Everyone who supports the child should uphold the values of person-centred planning and consider the child's views; listening to them and allowing them to make decisions about how they would like to be supported.

Person-centred planning is more than just a definition of need as it includes the person's aspirations. It is concerned with the whole person, not just education services. It asks questions about how they want to lead their life, how people can work with them to achieve this, and what help is needed.

There are five key features of person-centred planning.

> The person is at the centre.

> There is partnership working with the child's family, whose contribution is recognised and valued.

> It looks at what is important to the person now and in the future and identifies the support they need.

> It is an ongoing process with everyone working together to improve a person's quality of life.

> It should be a continual process of listening to the individual and taking action to enable the person to achieve their aims.

Many students receive help and support in school without an education, health and care plan. Additional SEN support in school is provided to enable students to meet their individual goals.

We have included a range of resources which we hope you will find useful in developing a profile of students.

Creating a thorough profile of each student with autism is vital to enable staff to find resources and activities that motivate them and reduce barriers to learning.

Appendices 1–5 are described below.

> **Appendix 1: profile for an older child** (page 42): a student profile should ideally be completed for all students who have autism. This provides a quick reference for all staff that come into contact with students and is particularly helpful for supply staff. The addition of a photograph clearly identifies which student the information relates to.

> **Appendix 2: example of a completed profile for an older child** (page 43)

> **Appendix 3: initial assessment chart** (page 44): this assessment looks in detail at possible barriers for learning and highlights areas to prioritise in each student's individual education plan or personalised plan.

> **Appendix 4: individual learning plan** (page 46): this plan breaks skills down into manageable chunks and makes it easier to identify the next step in learning.

> **Appendix 5: IEP target bank** (page 51): this resource contains lots of examples of targets suitable for inclusion in each student's individual education plan (IEP) or personalised plan. There is space to record details of issues and add additional targets.

You can find the appendices on pages 41-81.

3. The learning environment and the school day

The learning environment

These are some ways to help students with autism get used to the learning environment.

> Ensure that students' form tutors and subject teachers know that particular students have an autism spectrum disorder, giving them useful background to the condition. This can help them make arrangements to include the students in daily school life with the least possible disruption.

> Give each student with autism a clear map of the whole school (colour coded if possible) showing all areas. Students with an ASD often learn better with visual prompts (see Chapter 5). A map is a useful reference guide for all school students. Mark those areas that are 'out of bounds', for example school kitchens and teachers' resource areas. This should avoid students being anxious unnecessarily as all school buildings are clearly identified.

> Try to ensure that this map is displayed around the school; include a note identifying where the child currently is, with an arrow pointing 'YOU ARE HERE'.

> Specific areas and rooms should be labelled so students know which lesson takes place there and the kind of behaviour expected (for example sports changing rooms, art studio).

> Reminders of expected behaviour, especially rules relating to safety, should be clearly displayed next to specific equipment. Rules for general classroom behaviour could also be displayed on a class noticeboard. To ensure understanding, these rules could include visual reminders. Remember to state clearly what to do, rather than tell students what not to do, for example rather than saying 'don't run', give the instruction to walk.

Chapter 3: The learning environment and the school day

> Students are likely to benefit from having access to a work space that is free from unnecessary items as these may be extremely distracting.

> Students may be unusually sensitive to noise, lighting and so on, which others may not even notice. It may be helpful to find out exactly what is causing increased sensitivity. Although it can sometimes be difficult to eliminate such distractions, it is important to be aware that these may affect students' ability to concentrate.

> Finding places to sit or work can often be stressful – it may be useful to identify sitting and working areas in advance and keep them consistent if possible.

> Similarly, if group work is required, it may be useful to plan in the names of children who are suitable for a particular activity in advance, and keep this the same throughout a project or even the school year. It is a good idea to assign students with autism-specific roles within a group and to identify the rules associated with group work.

> It is helpful if resources are clearly labelled and accessible. Remember that it may be stressful for students with autism to negotiate a busy area of a classroom with lots of other students, which could lead to inappropriate or challenging behaviour associated with anxiety and frustration.

> The social elements associated with the learning environment should be made as obvious as possible. For example: when, how and where to store coats, and how to gain access to lockers.

The school day

Students with autism find the school day a lot easier if regular routines can be established, as routine helps to reduce anxiety often associated with social demands. A visual timetable can help establish the routine (see Chapter 5, page 21).

Students may need to be taught how and from whom to get help during the day. This information may need to be explicit to avoid them making an excessive number of visits to the school office.

Students benefit from having a general strategy in place to deal with sudden changes or emergencies. This could be established with the help of the SENCO and/or a teaching assistant.

Throughout the school day, adequate warnings and explanations should be given for transition periods as these can be stressful times. Students with autism often lack flexibility and so find change difficult. Do not expect students to be able to switch lessons suddenly and orientate themselves for a new activity automatically.

Lessons and/or room changeover times need to be planned for. It would be helpful if support could be put into place. For example, a teaching assistant could initially accompany students until a routine has been established. As students become more confident, the 'buddy' system could be used to ensure they know where to go and what to do next. This can be particularly effective if older students team up with those who are new to the school.

Consider letting students leave lessons early, or at least very promptly, to avoid having to rush and deal with large numbers of other students. This reduces social demands and may alleviate any unnecessary behaviour incidents that could arise from anxiety.

Some students with autism may perceive situations very differently from 'neurotypical' people. They can become anxious and constantly raise minor issues about their experience at school or the experiences of others.

If students often complain about issues that are not serious it may be worthwhile to provide them with a book for recording what is troubling them and monitoring their book with them at a designated time. This should cut down on unnecessary interruptions.

If there are times of high anxiety in the school day, for example lunchtimes, an easily accessible safe room or area could be planned in advance so there is some refuge from demanding situations. Ideally this should be offered in the learning support department as staff in this department are likely to be aware of students' needs. They can also help in times of stress by supporting students back into lessons.

Students may need reminding about acceptable behaviour during unstructured times of the school day. This could involve telling them a Social Story™ to deal with lengthy delays in the canteen. Social Stories™ are described in Chapter 7 (page 33).

Persistent and repetitive questioning may be a sign of a student's' need for reassurance about the school day. If this happens it is helpful to refer students to their timetable or Social Story™ and to emphasise that all the information is available and questioning should not be necessary.

The importance of taking responsibility for following a timetable may need to be emphasised. This is particularly important when students first encounter the secondary school system and again at the beginning of each new school year.

Students may benefit from reminders about timekeeping because they can become absorbed in a particular activity, especially if it relates to any special interest they might have. Using a countdown or timers before transitions often helps students with autism to manage moving from one activity to another.

To help students in secondary schools organise their belongings it is useful to have areas for them to use to store belongings and checklists to remind them of the resources required on particular days or for specific subjects.

The symbols shown in **Appendix 6** (page 67) may be useful for students with autism who require additional support to enable them to cope with transition and changes to the school day or staffing. The symbols can be photocopied and laminated.

Unstructured times

Times that are less structured, such as lunch and breaks, can cause some students anxiety. Places for students to go to and activities that are available could be discussed and agreed with students' key workers or staff from the learning support department. Each student's choice could be written next to the laminated symbol to ensure that they know what to do during free time. **Appendix 7** (page 58) shows some symbols to support unstructured times.

4. Accessing the curriculum

The curriculum may need to be differentiated to some degree for students with autism, not necessarily to make tasks 'easier' but to present learning tasks with a greater deal of clarity. Most students with autism need structure. Ways to enable students with autism to access the curriculum are discussed below.

Make the task clear

It is important to take steps to make sure tasks are as clear as possible to students with autism.

Adequate motivation can be extremely important, so tell students at the start if rewards or motivators are in place.

Do not assume that students can read social clues, so ensure that tasks are absolutely clear, for example, if notes are to be taken. Even if it seems that some tasks are obvious it is important to understand that body language, intonation and implicit references are likely to be missed; this can appear like negative or obstructive behaviour.

Students are likely to have difficulty generalising between subjects. Remember to make any connections explicit, even if it seems unnecessary at the time.

Problem solving and organisation can be particularly difficult. It may be necessary to introduce a writing frame or similar visual framework to reduce the demands of language.

As far as possible, try to avoid using sarcasm, irony and idioms because students with autism are likely to have a literal understanding of language. Give instructions in the order in which they are to be carried out. For example, try not to use sentences starting with: 'Before you do…'.

Students with autism can find it difficult to engage and maintain attention so it is important to point out the times when a student is expected to listen and retain the information given to them.

Remember to address students by name, as they might not realise that 'everybody' or 'the class' actually applies to them! Do this sensitively to avoid singling students out.

Ample opportunities for practical activities are of enormous benefit to students, who often find concrete 'hands on' activities easier to understand than text.

Use as many ways as possible to support work visually, for example diagrams, charts and time lines (see examples in the section in Chapter 5 called 'Using visuals to teach rules'), as many people with autism are visual thinkers. Visual maps can be used for students to record their ideas and enable them to organise their thoughts and develop understanding.

It may be necessary to teach students key vocabulary and concepts, and how to take notes during lessons. Displaying key vocabulary in the classroom or in students' books may well be beneficial to a large number of mainstream secondary students.

Make it very clear if students are expected to work within a group, and bear in mind the extreme social demands that are often implicit within the curriculum. Where possible, strike a balance between socially and academically demanding tasks. It may be helpful to assign students with autism a specific role within groups.

Remember to explain and model what you would like students to do, rather than tell them what not to do. In activities that rely heavily on teamwork, especially PE or games, provide explicit rules (visual, if possible, to avoid any ambiguities in language).

Provide structure

The following are some ways to provide structure to students with autism.

Students are likely to find any social environment a confusing and unpredictable place. Introducing structure to tasks generally alleviates anxiety.

> Students may introduce their own routines to enable them to cope with lessons. If these routines are acceptable then maintain them. If students' routines are obstructive, consider replacing them with another more positive routine.

> Many ASD students benefit from being given a complete overview of the topics or subjects they learn about, and a breakdown and explanation of the chunks of learning coming up in a lesson. This can be presented visually – see Chapter 5 (page 21).

> Ensure that activities have an obvious start and finish by defining the amount of work to be done or the amount of time to be spent on a particular task.

> If a particular activity involves several steps, list each step so students can progress through the work in a logical order.

> If a task is expected to be carried out over a few sessions, provide students with some idea of how long the task will last and what should be accomplished in each session. Once the task in hand is absolutely clear to them, many students work best independently, so try to plan for as many independent working opportunities as possible.

> To avoid students becoming anxious when presented with choices always explain every aspect of a lesson – state the obvious, and allow students plenty of time to make decisions. It may be necessary to offer a forced alternative, such as: "There are only two choices. Choose to do _____ or _____ ").

> Remember to consider the positive effects of organising the classroom or learning environment. See Chapter 3 (page 15).

Chapter 4: Accessing the curriculum

> Many students do not automatically know what resources they need, so provide a list.

> Make homework diaries as clear as possible – remember that subtle, implicit expectations may not have been understood.

The following photocopiable resources are designed to provide structured and explicit support to help students with organisation:

> **Appendix 8: lesson notes framework** (page 59)

> **Appendix 9: homework diary** (page 60)

> **Appendix 10: lesson notes framework and prompt list** (page 61)

Use a lesson notes framework

Students may be overwhelmed by the prospect of having to take notes during lessons.

The lesson notes framework shown in **Appendix 8** is designed so that students can begin to make a note of the important aspects of learning. It could be completed with the help of support staff if necessary. The lesson notes framework is designed so that students can eventually use this type of format independently. The last section entitled 'Questions or clarification' should be used in order to avoid interruptions to the teacher who is presenting the lesson.

Use homework diaries

Homework diaries may be filled in with help from support staff. **Appendix 9** shows an example homework diary, which can be used to record all the homework that students need to complete on one page. The subject and member of staff who has set and will mark the work are clearly identified. Noting down the topic provides the student with the context of the work to be completed. There is a space to list any resources that students might need in order to complete a task. The task can then be broken down into manageable steps and students can see when the work needs to be completed. Students should be able to complete homework independently once this approach has been introduced. See **Appendix 9** and **Appendix 10** for tools to help with this.

5. Using a visual approach

Why use a visual approach to autism?

Temple Grandin, who has autism, wrote:

I think in pictures. Words are like a second language to me. I translate both spoken and written words into full colour movies, complete with sound, which runs like a VCR [video cassette recorder] tape in my head. When somebody speaks to me, his words are instantly translated into pictures.
Grandin (2006, p3)

Although not all people with autism are such highly visual thinkers, research suggests that students with autism are consistently better at carrying out visual-spatial tasks than verbal and sequencing ones.

There are various ways of introducing visuals to support organisation.

Visual timetables

Timetables enable students to:

> follow the structure of the day without relying on verbal instructions or social cues

> have a point of continual reference to reduce anxiety and give them confidence and security

> avoid confrontation with adults – if it is time for an unpopular activity adults should refer students to the timetable "The timetable says that we are going to do..."

> reduce their questions about events in the day

> be prepared for changes

> link expected behaviours with timetabled activities

> develop independence by reducing reliance on adults giving and/or repeating verbal instructions.

Chapter 5: Using a visual approach

Implementing timetables with visual symbols

Some students may require the additional support of visual symbols to enable them to cope with lesson changeover times and changes to the day or staffing.

Appendix 11 (page 62) includes timetable symbols which can be reproduced. These can be especially helpful for younger students. Many teenagers with Asperger syndrome wish to blend in and do not want to be different from their peers, and it is important to be discreet when working with these students.

Most secondary schools provide diaries or planners but they vary in clarity. When students are stressed some may find it difficult to follow them, especially if there is a two week rolling programme. In these situations a daily timetable on a separate strip may help. These should be prepared by each student's key worker or the learning support department. To save time it is easier to arrange the daily symbols and photocopy and laminate them for one day and then if any changes are necessary they can be marked with a dry wipe marker pen.

Each student's key worker, SENCO or staff from the learning support department should run through the timetable at the beginning of the day explaining any room changes or changes of staffing.

Initially it may be necessary for the timetable to be referred to throughout the day. This helps students to understand the pattern of the day and teaches them to refer to the timetable independently.

An alternative way to present a visual timetable is to laminate the symbol sheets. Cut out and order the ones needed for that day. The cards can be joined with a treasury tag or put on a key fob. The advantage of this method is that the timetable is easily accessible and yet not obvious, as the cards fit into a pocket.

An example of a visual timetable:

A pocket-sized timetable:

Although visual timetables involve some effort to set up they are invaluable for students who find transition very stressful, as they provide structure and much needed confidence. Visual timetables can easily be kept in a pocket or bag without causing embarrassment to the students concerned.

Work schedules

Work schedules enable students to:

> know what work they are supposed to do, how much work there is, the order in which it is to be done, and what happens when it is finished

> build positive routines

> work independently

> feel a sense of achievement

> understand a set of instructions.

Many people with autism have organisational difficulties but when given a structure are very good at following it. This gives them the confidence to work more independently. In many curriculum subjects it is helpful if the supporting adult can quickly list the order of work that is expected from students during the session. See **Appendix 12: order of tasks** (page 63).

There are lesson frameworks and homework frameworks in Chapter 4 (page 18). Using these ensures that students understand exactly what is expected of them.

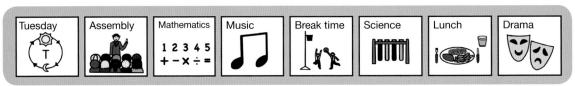

Use visuals to teach rules

A visual approach:

> removes the need for the students to be solely reliant on auditory input, which leads to a better understanding of the concept being taught

> appears to give students more confidence and independence

> reduces anxiety as the visual is a constant point of reference and students are not reliant on the adult for explanations

> reduces the number of questions relating to tasks.

Teach ways to record and organise knowledge and ideas visually

Teaching students to record and organise their ideas visually enables them to structure their thinking and make connections between ideas.

Consider using visual frameworks in lessons rather than giving students a blank piece of paper and expecting them to organise their own work. Visual organisers help to clarify thinking and understanding. Students with autism may have difficulty approaching tasks but can often follow an existing structure.

The Appendices include various examples of visual organisers which will enable students to make connections between pieces of information. These can be used across the secondary curriculum.

There are many uses for each of the suggested templates. Once students have learned how to organise their ideas into a template they can be encouraged to apply the technique in a variety of curriculum areas. The learning support department can play a vital role in supporting study skills by introducing visual organisation to students to support different subject areas. These tools can also be used to support assessment. The bank of visual templates can be photocopied and enlarged if necessary by the learning support department and disseminated to subject teachers.

Story planner

A story planner template can help a student construct a story in English or retell an historical event:

For a photocopiable story planner see **Appendix 13** (page 64).

Chapter 5: Using a visual approach

Experiment organiser

This template clearly lays out what steps need to be taken and describes how a conclusion has been reached.

This is especially helpful in science, geography and technology. It is particularly useful for students to use when looking to see what the problem is and to show current understanding from the outset.

The example below can be used alongside a science experiment.

For a photocopiable experiment organiser see **Appendix 15** (page 66).

Experiment organiser example: Venn diagrams

This template can be used to compare and contrast a variety of information, for example styles of poetry or art:

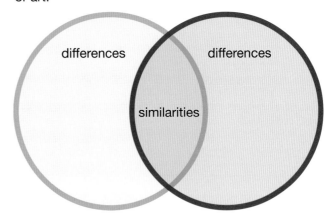

For a photocopiable Venn diagram see **Appendix 14** (page 65).

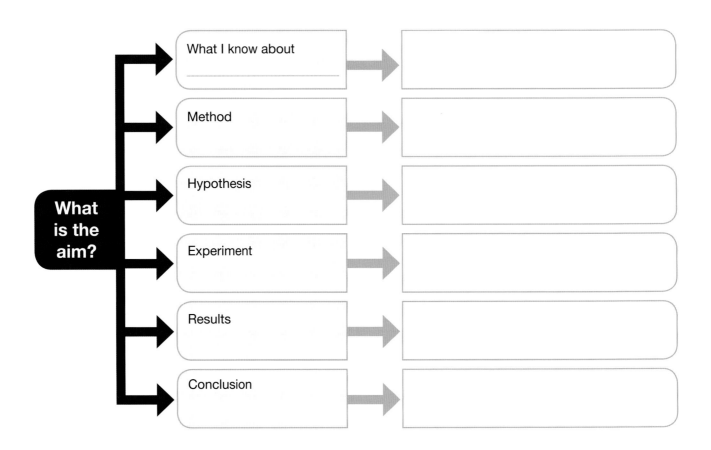

Problem solver

This template is similar in design to the organiser but uses different prompts to enable students to solve problems in a systematic way. The following example can be used alongside a mathematical problem:

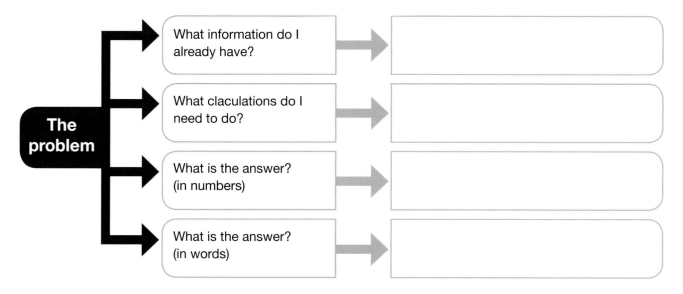

For a photocopiable problem solver see **Appendix 16** (page 67).

English or history organiser

This template is designed to clearly show the main elements of a story or factual event. This example shows a breakdown of the sequence of events in a story or historical episode:

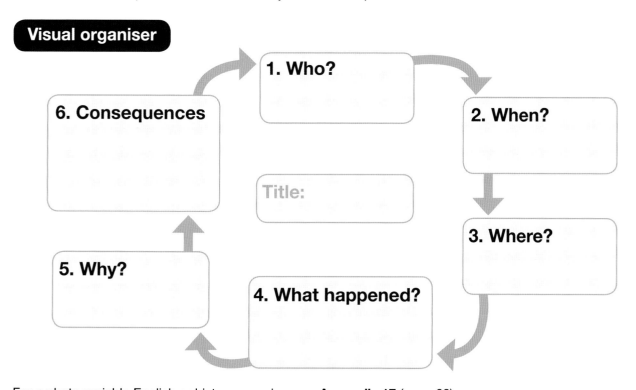

For a photocopiable English or history organiser see **Appendix 17** (page 68).

Chapter 5: Using a visual approach

Independent learning organiser

Once a suitable topic has been identified students can begin to manage their learning independently. This is particularly important for students with autism who can become reliant on the support of teaching assistants.

This example is useful for a geography topic:

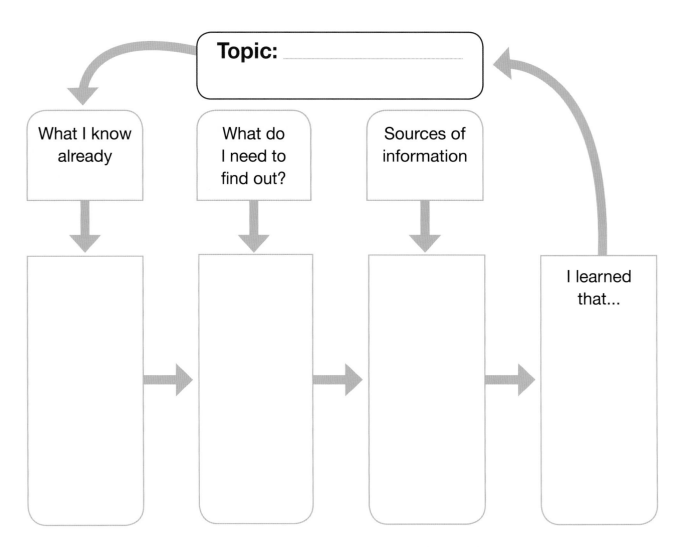

For a photocopiable independent learning organiser see **Appendix 18** (page 69).

Making a balanced decision

This template is helpful when students are developing ideas and considering their consequences. This example could be used when considering topics in citizenship:

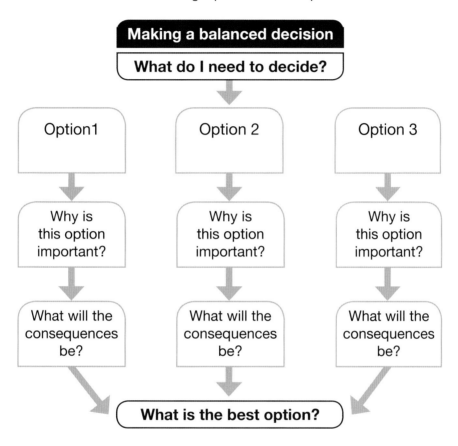

For a photocopiable 'making a balanced decision' template see **Appendix 19** (page 70).

Considering both sides of an argument

Students with autism often have a black and white view of the world and find it difficult to consider more than one side to an argument. This visual organiser can be used in any subject to extend their thinking and can be used across the curriculum.

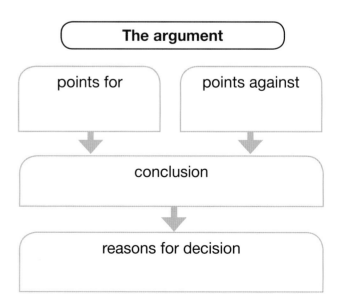

For a photocopiable 'sides of an argument' template see **Appendix 20** (page 71).

Chapter 5: Using a visual approach

Teaching visual mapping

Students with autism often focus on small details and have difficulty seeing an overview. Making thinking visual is sometimes known as concept mapping, model mapping or Mind Mapping®.

The terms 'Mind Map®' and 'Mind Mapping®' are registered trademarks of the Buzan Organisation Ltd, which uses a combination of key words, colour and visual images to record everything that can be remembered about a particular topic on a single sheet of paper. Tony Buzan described a Mind Map® as:

> **The easiest way to put information into your brain and to take information out of your brain – it's a creative and effective means of note-taking that literally 'maps out' your thoughts.**
> Buzan (2002, p6)

Visual maps:

> enable students to have an overview of a topic and how everything fits together, and help students to see the 'whole picture'

> help students make sense and meaning out of their thoughts

> require students to think about how to arrange information, organise their thoughts and develop understanding

> use colour and visual images so more of the brain is involved in the learning process

> show how students are learning and indicate gaps in their learning.

Example of a visual map:

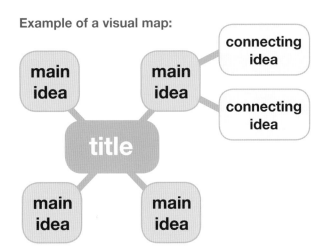

To construct a visual map:

> write the title of the topic in the centre of the paper or (preferably) draw a picture

> start to build the visual map by drawing lines off from the title; write down one main idea on each line; draw more lines for any key words you associate with that idea

> repeat with other ideas and key words, although visual images can be substituted for key words; they are more easily remembered than words

> use a different colour for each idea.

Students with autism may have difficulty connecting ideas. Working with an adult or one of their peers will help them to clarify their ideas and develop their understanding.

Some students find it helpful to brainstorm ideas and write the words on 'stick on' notes. These can then be sorted and organised into a visual map. To begin with, students may need to sort prepared pictures if they cannot come up with their own ideas.

Visual maps are a particularly useful strategy for:

> Assessment. If pupils make an individual visual map at the beginning of the topic and again at the end it allows the adult to have an insight into what and how they think.

> Prompting communication. When pupils have completed their visual map, they can then use it to help them to clarify their thoughts during discussion.

> Reinforcing concepts. Make a visual map as a class or group and then ask pupils to make a visual map individually.

For more information on mind mapping see Tony Buzan's helpful book **'How to Mind Map'** (2002).

The computer program 'Thinking with Pictures' (see Information Sources, pages 37-39) has a range of visual tools including concept maps, mind maps, webs, trees and bubble maps. Another tool which may be useful is the 'Smart Art' facility in Microsoft Word.

6. Promoting positive behaviour

It is not always easy to work out the reason for a behaviour but it is important to try to identify the function of an undesirable behaviour so you know how to respond in a way that will help to reduce future instances of it. It is worth considering that the same behaviour can serve different functions for different pupils.

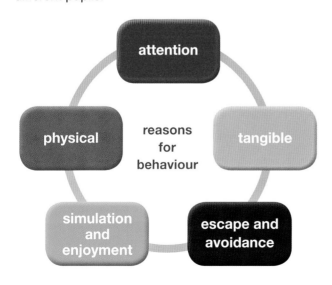

Undesirable behaviour

These are some of the reasons why a student with autism might demonstrate undesirable behaviour.

> **For physical reasons**. It is important to rule out any medical factors that might be causing negative behaviour such as a headache or toothache. It is also worth considering if behaviour is caused by physical discomfort such as tiredness or hunger.

> **To seek attention**. A student might behave in a certain way to get attention or a response from an adult or their peers.

> **To achieve something**. Students may exhibit certain behaviours to get an object they want or to be allowed to carry out an alternative activity to the one they might be engaged in.

Chapter 6: Promoting positive behaviour

> **To escape or avoid something**. Sometimes students behave in a particular way to avoid an activity or situation, such as a task set by the teacher or a social situation they want to get away from. Students with autism may fear things that most of us would not find frightening, for example, the noise of hand dryers. They might be afraid when they do not know what to expect, so changes in routine or transitions can cause anxiety.

> **For stimulation and enjoyment**. Some students with autism are sensory seeking, for example they may rock, flap their hands or watch patterns of light in order to obtain the right amount of sensory feedback or stimulation. If the behaviour is considered inappropriate try to find socially acceptable and safe ways for students to find the desired sensory stimulation.

Always look for positive behaviour that could serve the same function as negative behaviour. It is important to praise positive behaviour.

Promoting positive behaviour in the classroom

Each student with autism would benefit from having a named key worker in order to establish a positive relationship and oversee any social or academic areas that may be causing problems.

In order to prevent unnecessary conflict, each member of staff who deals with students with autism should be well informed. There is an example of a student profile in the appendices (pages 42-43). This profile may be used to give all staff an accessible overview of each individual student with a diagnosis of autism.

In addition to the profile, all staff should have each student's individual education plan (IEP) to refer to. This gives school staff information and strategies and enables staff to address students' social and academic needs consistently. It is incredibly beneficial to use a consistent approach when working with students with autism, who generally lack social understanding.

Students with autism can usually be easily motivated by rewards, especially if they relate to their special interests; the traditional rewards used for students who are not on the spectrum do not necessarily engage those with autism. Children we have worked with have been motivated by collecting paper clips, used stamps and looking at plumbing systems around the school with the site manager!

Rewards and motivating activities that are based on a numbered or structured system tend to be especially accessible and supportive for students with autism. These types of behaviour systems are clearly understood by staff and students and remove any arbitrary judgements about behaviour.

Because motivation and clear boundaries are so important, ideally rewards and sanctions should be planned well in advance and need to be in place from the first day. State clearly what students' rewards will be and how they can be earned. Similarly, unacceptable behaviour needs to be identified, even if this seems to be stating the obvious. Sanctions need to be made clear.

Students with autism can benefit from visual warnings if their behaviour is inappropriate – often verbal language used by adults is too complex for them to process effectively, especially if they are anxious. Avoid any discussions about behaviour until they are calm and able to reflect on what has happened.

Expected behaviour should always be displayed clearly in areas around the school. It is always important to state the behaviour that you expect rather than label the behaviour that you do not wish to see.

Students should be prepared for any specific parts of the school or activities that may trigger unwanted behaviour, such as lengthy queues in the canteen.

Consider using a quiet, distraction free room or area where students could be taken in order to have time out if lessons become too stressful, for example a learning support unit or small withdrawal room. It is important that this is a designated area and made familiar to students in advance so they are always fully aware of about where they are being taken and why.

If students are unsure about where they are going, it is likely to cause additional stress and may not reduce unwanted behaviour. This area could also be used at break times if this is a source of difficulty.

Ensure that students have their own timetable and if necessary a Social Story™, which is easily accessible and portable, for example, using cards on a treasury tag.

Remember, always to try to make instructions as clear and specific as possible – never be afraid to state the obvious. When speaking to a student begin by saying the student's name so they know to listen. Tell them what to do rather than what not to do – it is more beneficial to give guidance. For example, say, "James, please hang your coat up outside the room on the peg", rather than "James, don't put your coat on the desk". Many occurrences of misbehaviour start when students with autism misinterpret instructions or fail to see the relevance and misunderstand completely.

Use visual cards to alert staff that students are experiencing particular difficulties and need help. This eliminates any immediate demands that may be placed on speech and language. Language disorders generally become more prominent in times of stress.

The ABC of behaviour

Challenging behaviour is not necessary physical or verbal aggression – it covers a range of behaviours including passive behaviour and self-harming. To identify possible triggers for a particular behaviour use the ABC of behaviour.

> A = Antecedent. Record what happened before the challenging behaviour occurred. Consider factors such as interactions with adults and peers, any possible sensory overload, possible environmental reasons and the time the behaviour occurred.

> B = Behaviour. Describe details of the incident and who was involved.

> C= Consequences. Record what happened after the event and think about what the behaviour achieved for each pupil.

The ABC of behaviour:

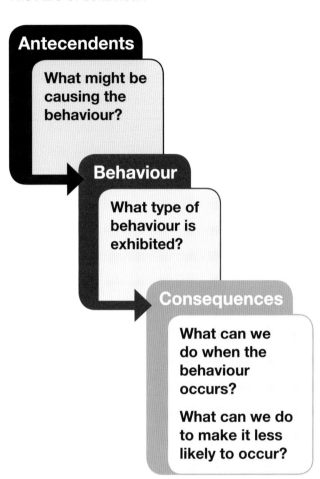

The following resources may be useful to promote positive behaviour.

> **Appendix 21: observation chart** (page 72)

> **Appendix 22: angry arrow chart** (page 73)

> **Appendix 23: example of a completed angry arrow chart** (page 74)

> **Appendix 24: individual behaviour cards** (page 75)

> **Appendix 25: behaviour chart to develop motivation** (page 76)

> **Appendix 26: example of a completed behaviour support plan** (page 77)

> **Appendix 27: blank behaviour support plan** (page 78).

Chapter 6: Promoting positive behaviour

Teaching coping strategies

Students with autism often have difficulty recognising their feelings. It is important to help them recognise when they are angry and to spot the situations that can induce anger. When they are calm, teach coping strategies. Explain that it is okay to feel angry but not okay to react in such a way that others get hurt, property gets damaged or they harm themselves.

Make a plan with students that details what they will do when they become angry to reduce their stress.

These are some ways to help students to calm down:

> identify a quiet place that they could go to

> teach them to take deep breaths and count to ten

> put together a box of items that the student particularly likes or create a book of favourite images that the student can look at when angry

> identify an adult the student can talk to

> encourage the student to take some physical exercise

> encourage the student to get involved in a favourite activity such as drawing, colouring or reading a favourite book.

Use **Appendix 22: angry arrow chart** (page 73) to record the steps students should try to take towards becoming calm. **Appendix 23** (page 74) shows an example of a completed angry arrow chart.

Individual behaviour cards

Cards that can be shown when a student is out of control or overwhelmed by a situation can prove very effective and help avoid unnecessary confrontation with students by unfamiliar adults.

The cards should describe the difficulties students face and coping strategies. These are obviously individual to each student and the cards could be designed and written by them. See **Appendix 24: individual behaviour cards** (page 74).

> I have autism.
>
> I may get into a panic.
>
> When I get into a panic I find it difficult to understand speech.
>
> I am very sensitive to sounds.
>
> Please do not touch me.
>
> Please do not stand too close.
>
> Please do not shout.

Angry — Walk away — Count to 10 — Go to my quiet place — Draw some cartoons — Calm

7. Developing social relationships

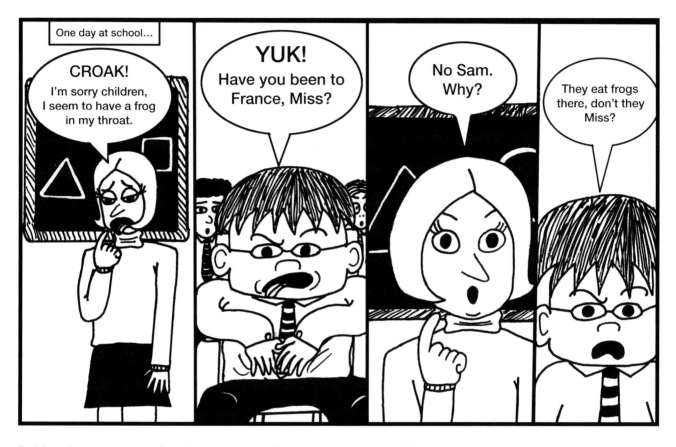

Raising the awareness of autism among staff and other students in the school is crucial. Plan and deliver sessions for raising awareness, where appropriate, with outside agencies that offer specialist support. This could be done within personal, social and health education (PSHE) or school assemblies for students and during staff meetings or INSET for staff.

Staff should be aware that students with autism could be vulnerable to teasing by other students, especially if they have different or unusual interests. Students with autism may not be aware that other students are teasing or being unkind so staff need to be vigilant and look out for this type of behaviour.

Students may prefer not to socialise at break times and often benefit from learning and practising social skills and socially acceptable behaviour in a variety of more structured contexts.

Ongoing social skills groups are of great benefit for students with autism as a forum in which to discuss and learn new social skills, and explore more acceptable outcomes to negative behaviour. Where possible these groups should include positive role models. This book includes tried and tested resources and references to books that can guide the planning of a social skills group within the school.

Students with autism often have little social awareness, no tact and may say exactly what they are thinking! Staff and peers need to be made aware of students' difficulties so they can understand and make allowances. Each student's key worker can give guidance and support and work with the student on acceptable and appropriate comments.

Students with autism are often unaware of personal space and may stand too close to other people, which can make them feel threatened or uncomfortable. They may not make eye contact or may hold eye contact for too long. These social skills, which other students pick up automatically, need to be explained and taught to students with autism.

Chapter 7: Developing social relationships

Social stories

Students with autism may misunderstand the intentions of other students or misinterpret social situations. This can be the cause of negative behaviour. It is often helpful to address such situations clearly; using Social Stories™ can help.

The idea of Social Stories™ has been developed by Carol Gray. She describes what they are in the introduction to **'My Social Stories Book'**:

> **A Social Story™ is a process that results in a product. As a process, parents and professionals consider the perspective of the child while describing a situation, skill, or concept in terms of relevant social clues, perspectives, and common responses. Each Social Story™ is developed according to specific guidelines that are based on the learning characteristics of children with ASD.**
> Gray (2002, p17)

Social Stories™ can:

> describe social situations and appropriate behaviour without the usual teacher and pupil interaction

> teach routines and help pupils cope with changes

> break down situations into small, understandable steps

> help pupils overcome negative behaviour, such as aggression, fear and obsession

> help pupils understand and cope with a forthcoming event

> help pupils cope with new situations.

Sharing Social Stories™ helps pupils to learn that everyone has the same expectations. Other adults can refer to the Social Story™ and help pupils when they encounter a difficulty.

For more information on writing a Social Story™ and examples, see Carol Gray's helpful book **'My Social Stories Book'** (2002).

8. Supporting transition

Transition checklists

Children with autism usually need support when they prepare for a totally new environment or experience. As a result of difficulties associated with change and the unpredictability of new situations, transition from nursery school to primary and primary to secondary school can be traumatic times. Staff may find that adequate preparation for entry to a new school prevents a great deal of anxiety for the child and the staff who will be working with them! This chapter outlines plans for successful transition that can be followed to enable the process to be as smooth as possible.

Appendix 28 (page 79) provides a transition checklist for a student transferring from primary to secondary school.

Transitions from activity to activity

Any change can result in students with autism becoming anxious. Strategies described earlier such as visual timetables and individual schedules can reduce this anxiety.

Sand timers

Showing students a sand timer to give a warning of a change can be helpful. Use a timer that indicates different spans of time. It is useful to have some with a short time such as 30 seconds and others with longer times.

Activity transition symbols

Using a visual such as a traffic light which students are very familiar with can be a useful strategy to help them cope with change and transition times.

The meaning of the colours of a traffic light:

Green means an activity is starting

Yellow means get ready to stop

Red means time to stop

Show the yellow symbol to students when it is nearly time to stop an activity. Some students also require the use of a sand timer too to help them cope with the change of activity. When showing the red symbol (meaning it is time to stop) show students a symbol of the activity you wish them to move on to.

Transitions from school or college to work

Secondary school or college is a time to prepare students with autism for their adult life. It is important to start to discuss what types of work students might like to do as these discussions are very useful to students and help them to be successful in later life. Many students with autism may see school or college as an isolated experience rather than as preparation for work.

Some students with autism may have unrealistic expectations about their future career choice. Others may not be aware of their strengths or that some of their talents are especially useful for some types of employment. A good place to start transition planning is to draw up a list of preferred careers, then establish strengths, interests and challenges that individual students have. The ideal careers for each student are a balance of strengths, interests and just the right level of challenge.

Chapter 8: Supporting transition

Students need to understand the different types of careers they may be able to access and that they may need to have additional qualifications if they wish to pursue certain careers. They may also need to learn that there are different ways to obtain qualifications, for example through online courses, job training with an employer and extra courses at college.

Students with autism probably need extra support with interviews as they rely heavily on social and communication skills, two areas that are inherently difficult for people with autism. Guide students to help them to make appropriate presentations by referring them to the job advert and application form.

Work experience is invaluable for students with autism, but students need adequate time to prepare for work and the workplace, and colleagues in the organisation should be carefully chosen to ensure that the experience is positive. Preparation for work experience, including visits, is very beneficial.

The key to successful transitions from school or college to work is to draw up a transition plan with students. Start the transition planning with each student's ultimate goal and then work backwards to enable the student to realise how school, college and work are connected.

See **Appendix 29: transition checklist from school or college to work**.

9. Information sources

Organisations

The National Autistic Society
393 City Road
London EC1V 1NG

020 7833 2299
www.autism.org.uk

The National Autistic Society produces a comprehensive publications catalogue and some very useful leaflets on autism and Asperger syndrome. It also runs an Autism Helpline (0808 800 4104) Monday – Friday, 10am-4pm. Local branches of the NAS run courses and conferences in your area so it may be worth getting in touch.

Parents can also be referred to the Parent to Parent Service (0808 800 4106). This service offers parents of children with autism the opportunity to speak in confidence to other parents. Calls are free landlines and most mobiles.

Autism Education Trust

c/o The National Autistic Society
393 City Road
London EC1V 1NG

020 7903 3650
www.autismeducationtrust.org

The Autism Education Trust helps raise awareness of the importance of appropriate educational provision for children and young people on the autism spectrum. The website has information about training opportunities, web-based resources and examples of good practice. There is a section on the website for children called 'Kids Zone', which contains information and games, and 'The Den', which is designed for teenagers.

Useful publications

Al-Ghani, K.I. (2010). Learning About Friendship: Stories to Support Social Skills Training in Children with Asperger Syndrome and High Functioning Autism. London: Jessica Kingsley.
This collection of illustrated stories explores friendship issues encountered by children with ASD aged four to eight and looks at how they can be overcome.

Attwood, T. (2008). The Complete Guide to Asperger's Syndrome. London: Jessica Kingsley.
Tony Attwood's considerable experience as a specialist in the field of Asperger syndrome makes this an authoritative book on the subject.

Baker, J. E. (2003). Social Skills Training For Children and Adolescents with Asperger Syndrome and Social-Communication Problems. London: Jessica Kingsley.
A comprehensive social skills training programme.

Beaney, J. (2013). Sensory Assessment and Intervention Programme. London: Speechmark.
This resource contains a sensory assessment and a bank of sensory activities.

Buzan, T. (2002) How to Mind Map. London: Thorsons.
A practical guide to mind mapping.

Cumine, V., Leach, J., and Stevenson G. (2009) Asperger Syndrome: A Practical Guide for Teachers. London: David Fulton.
This book provides effective educational and behavioural strategies to use in the classroom.

Frith, U. (2008). Autism: A Very Short Introduction. Oxford: OUP.
A well written, informative short guide.

Chapter 9: Sources of information

Grandin, T. (2006). Thinking in Pictures.
New York: Vintage.
This is a personal account of what it is like to think, feel and experience the world if you have autism.

Grandin, T. and Duffy, K. (2008). Developing talents: careers for individuals with Asperger syndrome and high-functioning autism. Kansas, USA. Autism Asperger Publishing.
This book contains useful strategies and ideas to help individuals on the spectrum find jobs and careers.

Gray, C. (2002). My Social Story Book.
London: Jessica Kingsley.
Social stories are very effective in teaching social skills. The book provides many examples of social stories and is a useful guide if you want to try writing your own.

Hall, K. (2000). Asperger syndrome, the universe and everything. London: Jessica Kingsley.
This book is helpful to teenagers with Asperger syndrome and also for others working with them. Kenneth has Asperger syndrome and he describes the difficulties he had at school. This photocopiable resource offers a flexible framework for the assessment and measurement of the communication skills of children with autism spectrum disorders.

Jackson, L. (2002). Freaks, geeks and Asperger syndrome. London: Jessica Kingsley.
This book is written by a 13-year-old who has a diagnosis of Asperger syndrome. It is witty and helps others understand the difficulties teenagers face.

Kershaw, P. (2011). The ASD workbook: understanding your autism spectrum disorder. London: Jessica Kingsley.
A diagnosis of an ASD can be confusing and overwhelming for all involved, and it can be difficult for parents to know the best way to approach the subject with their child. This easy-to-use interactive workbook gives parents the help they need to explain ASD to their child.

Lawson, W. (2000). Life behind glass.
London: Jessica Kingsley.
Wendy Lawson has an autism spectrum disorder and she has written about her feelings and experiences. The book gives an insight into what life can be like for those with autism spectrum disorder.

Lawson, W. (2010). The passionate mind.
London: Jessica Kingsley.
An interesting book in which Wendy Lawson explains autism in terms of the individual with autism's unique learning style.

Miller, L. (2009). Practical behaviour management solutions for children and teens with autism: the 5P approach. London: Jessica Kingsley.
This book is packed with practical, structured strategies and expert, flexible guidance to help someone support a child or young person on the autism spectrum.

The National Autistic Society (2003). Approaches to autism.
This guide outlines different approaches to autism and gives details of where to find out further information.

Ordetx, K. (2012). Teaching theory of mind.
London: Jessica Kingsley.
This book provides an easy-to-follow curriculum for teaching children with high-functioning autism or Asperger syndrome.

Painter, K. K. (2006). Social skills groups for children and adolescents with Asperger's syndrome. London: Jessica Kingsley.
This is a ready-to-use curriculum for practitioners who wish to lead social skills groups for children and adolescents with autism spectrum disorders.

Powell, S. (ed.) (2000). Helping children with autism to learn. Abingdon: David Fulton.
This book is a detailed guide to how children with autism think and learn and the approaches that can be used to teach them.

Silver, K. (2005). Assessing and developing communication and thinking skills in people with autism and communication difficulties. London: Jessica Kingsley.
This photocopiable resource offers a flexible framework for the assessment and measurement of the communication skills of children with autism spectrum disorders.

Vermeulen, P. (2001). Autistic thinking: this is the title. London: Jessica Kingsley.
This book looks at the ways people with autism think. It offers an insight into the very individual way in which people with autism process information.

Wilkes, K. (2005). The sensory world of the autistic spectrum: a greater understanding. London: The National Autistic Society.
An informative booklet giving an insight into sensory difficulties.

Willey, L. H. (2003). Asperger syndrome in adolescence: living with the ups, the downs and things in between. London: Jessica Kingsley.
This book aims to make the transition to adulthood as painless as possible.

Wing, L. (2006). What's so special about autism? London: The National Autistic Society.
A discussion of the characteristics of autism and how they affect the services that people with an autism spectrum disorder need.

DVDs

Asperger Syndrome: A Different Mind (2006), narrated by Simon Baron-Cohen. London: Jessica Kingsley.
This DVD looks at the nature of Asperger syndrome from the viewpoint of children and adults who have the condition, and their family members and school teachers.

Autism and Me (2007), by Rory Hoy. London: Jessica Kingsley.
This award-winning short film describes what it is like to have autism.

Computer software

Communicate: In Print. Available from www.widgit.com.
A desktop publishing program for creating symbol supported resources.

Symbols2Write. Available from iStore or at www.widgit.com.
A series of apps available for Apple and Microsoft platforms.

Widgit Go. Available from www.widgit.com.
An app available for Apple and Android platforms.

Thinking with Pictures. Available from Logotron Educational Software: www.r-e-m.co.uk.
Mind-mapping software.

Diagnostic criteria

ICD-10 (International Classification of Diseases), World Health Organization

DSM-V (Diagnostic & Statistical Manual), American Psychiatric Association

Appendices: photocopiable resources

Appendix 1: profile for an older child

PUPIL PROFILE			
Name:	**Class:**	**Year:**	**Date:**

Strengths:	Weaknesses:

Things I would like to be better at:	Things that will help me achieve my aims:

Appendix 2: example of a completed profile for an older child

PUPIL PROFILE				

Name: Tanya Soos   **Class:** 9P2   **Year:** 9   **Date:** 02/09/14

Strengths:	Weaknesses:
Friendly towards adults	Can be difficult to motivate in some lessons
Very motivated if task or topic is of interest	Easily bored
Can work in small groups	Can decide reward is 'not worth it'
Enjoys computer work	Becomes easily frustrated if task is perceived too difficult
Good range of interests	Becomes angry if situation is perceived as unfair
Good range of vocabulary	Tires quickly when doing handwriting
Initially motivated by rewards and sanctions	
Can display good social skills	

Things I would like to be better at:	Things that will help me achieve my aims:
Independent (of adult) tasks	Help to organise work
Creative writing	Adult support for writing tasks
Problem solving	Social skills group to work on developing friendship skills
Reading fluency and expression	Strategies to help with keeping calm
Keeping friends	
Controlling anger	

Appendix 3: initial assessment chart

Initial assessment				
Pupil's name:			**Date of assessment:**	
Please tick to indicate which of the child's difficulties are causing concern and creating a barrier to their learning.	Major difficulty	Difficulty	Causes some difficulty	Not a problem
Social relationships				
Difficulty making and sustaining friendships				
Seeks interaction but in an inappropriate way				
Prefers to play alone				
Inappropriate reactions to situations, eg laughs when others are upset				
Misinterprets other people's behaviour				
Low self-esteem				
Social communication				
Difficulty understanding instructions				
Delay in processing information				
Limited language skills				
Uses complex language but does not always understand meaning				
Takes things literally				
Difficulty understanding non-verbal communication				
Social imagination and flexibility of thought				
Difficulty generalising skills				
Difficulty with activities involving sequencing and prioritising				
Rigid thinking skills				
Poor organisational skills				
Difficulty recognising own feelings				
Difficulty understanding the feelings and thoughts of others				
Difficulty anticipating future events				
Difficulty coping with changes to routines				
Difficulty coping with new situations				
Transitions cause anxiety				
Has a narrow range of interests				
Has obsessions				

Initial assessment continued

Please tick to indicate which of the child's difficulties are causing concern and creating a barrier to their learning.	Major difficulty	Difficulty	Causes some difficulty	Not a problem
Sensory				
Hypersensitive to or displays abnormal reaction to:				
> visual stimuli				
> sounds				
> tastes				
> smells				
> textures				
Difficulty processing and interpreting information from senses				
High activity level				
Sometimes lacks motivation				
Development of skills				
Poor fine motor skills				
Poor penmanship skills				
Poor gross motor skills				
Delay in development of self-help skills				

Behaviour

Describe behaviours that are causing concern:

Other concerns

Describe any other concerns:

Appendix 4: individual learning plan

Skills have been broken down into small steps. Ideally the areas to target are a pupil's emerging skills.

Social communication

Verbal and expressive

1   Gains attention physically

2   Gains attention verbally

3   Communicates needs using object

4   Communicates needs using photo

5   Communicates needs using symbol

6   Communicates needs using sign

7   Repeats adults' words and phrases when prompted

8   Repeats children's words and phrases when prompted

9   Labels familiar objects

10 Makes verbal requests to communicate needs

11 Makes requests for preferred activities using object

12 Makes requests for preferred activities using photo

13 Makes requests for preferred activities using symbol

14 Makes requests for preferred activities using sign

15 Makes verbal requests for preferred activities

16 Signs hello and goodbye

17 Says hello and goodbye

18 Uses names of familiar adults

19 Uses names of familiar pupils

20 Answers questions:

   a. what?
   b. who?
   c. where?
   d. when?
   e. why?
   f. how?

21 Asks questions:

   a. what?
   b. who?
   c. where?
   d. when?
   e. why?
   f. how?

22 Volunteers information (eg about home, school etc.)

23 Can use narrative (can link ideas together coherently, eg in news time)

24 Uses verbal language to:

   a. comment
   b. give information
   c. seek information
   d. express feelings and thoughts
   e. negotiate
   f. compromise
   g. reason

25 Makes appropriate use of:

   a. tone
   b. rate
   c. volume
   d. intonation

26 Addresses others appropriately (eg friends, teachers)

27 Has topic maintenance

28 Has topic saliency

29 Is aware of age appropriate comments

30 Differentiates between adults and peers

31 Varies responses for audience (eg formal and non-formal)

32 Shared knowledge:

   a. states obvious
   b. omits key information
   c. assumes knowledge wrongly

Social communication

Verbal and receptive

1   Responds to own name

2   Acknowledges speaker: turns and looks

3   Responds to appropriate language requests made with objects

4   Responds to appropriate language requests made with photos

5   Responds to appropriate language requests made with symbols

6   Responds to appropriate language requests made with signs

7   Responds to appropriate verbal language requests

8   Demonstrates 'active listening' (sitting and standing still, looking at speaker, thinking about words, asking if unsure)

9   Monitors own comprehension

10 Understands:

   a. humour
   b. sarcasm
   c. figurative speech
   d. idioms
   e. inference
   f. deduction

Additional conversational skills

11 Takes turns in conversations

12 Has developed basic conversational reciprocity

13 Interrupts appropriately

14 Can join in an existing conversation appropriately

15 Can initiate conversations appropriately

16 Can close a conversation appropriately

17 Allows others to join conversations

18 Pauses in a conversation to allow others to speak

19 Repairs conversational breakdowns

Non-verbal skills

1   Can direct own attention to listening tasks within ability

2   Orientates towards speaker

3   Gives eye contact when speaking or signing

4   Gives eye contact when listening

5   Understands facial expressions:

   a. happy
   b. sad
   c. angry
   d. upset
   e. frightened
   f. worried
   g. excited

6   Uses facial expressions:

   a. happy
   b. sad
   c. angry
   d. upset
   e. frightened
   f. worried
   g. excited

7   Uses gesture to support meaning

8   Understands that gestures support meaning

9   Uses body language to support meaning

10 Understands that body language supports meaning

11. Monitors response of others

12 Monitors response of others and alters action accordingly

Social interaction

1   Aware of their own appearance, eg photo

2   Aware of others' appearance, eg photo

3   Aware of personal safety

4   Aware of the presence of others: adults

5   Aware of the presence of others: children

6   Tolerates others in same space or area: adults

7   Tolerates others in close proximity: children

8   Motivated to interact

9   Responds to finger pointing

Appendices

Social interaction continued

10 Establishes joint attention (can follow another's point of interest): children

11 Establishes joint attention (can follow another's point of interest): adults

12 Can use own resources in proximity to adults

13 Can use own resources in proximity to children

14 Can use same resources in proximity to adults

15 Can use same resources in proximity to children

16 Establishes shared reference (can maintain interest in same activity as another): adults

17 Establishes shared reference (can maintain interest in same activity as another): children

18 Can wait for requested activity or resource

19 Shares objects (can tolerate others having access to same set of resources): adults

20 Shares objects (can tolerate others having access to same set of resources): children

21 Takes turns with objects (can allow others to have exclusive use of same resource for a limited period): adults

22 Takes turns with objects (can allow others to have exclusive use of same resource for a limited period): children

23 Partially participates in one-to-one activities with adults

24 Partially participates in one-to-one activities with children

25 Participates in one-to-one activities with adults

26 Participates in one-to-one activities with children

27 Can initiate one-to-one interaction with adults

28 Can initiate one-to-one interaction with children

29 Can partially participate in small groups

30 Can fully participate in small groups

31 Can partially participate in large groups

32 Can fully participate in large groups

33 Can partially participate in whole school groups

34 Can fully participate in whole school groups

35 Maintains appropriate proximity towards others

36 Uses personal contact appropriately

37 Interprets personal contact appropriately

38 Shows interest in others' actions and behaviours

39 Can choose people to interact with

40 Collaborates on basic tasks

41 Follows explicit group rules

42 Follows implicit group rules

43 Terminates interaction appropriately

44 Tolerates others joining and leaving group

45 Understands consequences

46 Understands impact of own actions on others

47 Makes accurate assumptions about others' actions

48 Aware of explicit social conventions

49 Aware of implicit social conventions

Flexibility of thought and behaviour

Micro transitions

1 Travels with physical prompts between areas of the room

2 Travels with physical prompts between neighbouring rooms

3 Travels with physical prompts between areas of school

4 Travels with transition objects between areas of the room

5 Travels with transition objects between neighbouring rooms

6 Travels with transition objects between areas of school

7 Travels with visual prompts between areas of the room

8 Travels with visual prompts between neighbouring rooms

9 Travels with visual prompts between areas of school

10 Travels independently between areas of the room

11 Travels independently between neighbouring rooms

12 Travels independently between areas of school

Macro transitions

1   Can identify photo of current setting
2   Can identify photo of new setting
3   Knows (name of) current setting
4   Has visited new setting
5   Understands change of settings
6   Knows name of new setting
7   Knows specific environments
    (eg new class, art room)
8   Knows some new adults' names
9   Knows some new children's names
10 Knows when move will take place

Coping with change

1   Follows adult's positive routines
2   Can follow an object schedule or timetable
3   Can follow a photo schedule or timetable
4   Can follow a photo or symbol schedule
    or timetable
5   Can follow a symbol schedule or timetable
6   Can follow a symbol or written schedule
    or timetable
7   Can follow a written schedule or timetable
8   Able to finish a preferred activity
9   Can make transition to new activity
10 Ability to alter thoughts and behaviour

Problem solving

1   Able to choose from a forced alternative
2   Able to choose one item from three, four
    or five items
3   Understands concept of 'not available'
4   Understands something has gone wrong
5   Understands need for a solution
6   Searches for dropped item
7   Searches for missing item
8   Attempts appropriate solutions
9   Able to request help if needed

10 Can explain and/or demonstrate problem
11 Finds alternative solutions
12 Requests demonstration
13 Requests information
14 Understands if lost
15 Requests directions

Social imagination

1   Able to cease repetitive behaviour on request
    if redirected
2   Able to alter own routine if given alternatives
3   Able to confine special interests to an
    appropriate time
4   Able to suddenly alter actions, eg for a fire drill
    or other emergency
5   Understand if has physically hurt another person
    or animal
6   Can explore new resources
7   Can explore new areas in the classroom
8   Can engage in others' choices of activity
    or resource
9   Able to experience new environments within
    the school
10 Able to experience new environments outside
    of school
11 Able to predict what happens next
12 Understands if their actions may be dangerous
13 Has varied interests
14 Understands people have different interests
15 Able to separate fantasy and reality
16 Follows a play sequence
17 Imitates others' play
18 Uses play materials repetitively
19 Uses play materials functionally
20 Uses play materials symbolically
21 Uses play materials creatively
22 Extends play ideas
23 Develops own play ideas
24 Varies use of play and leisure materials
25 Can create play sequences with other people

Appendices

Independence

1   Moves between activities without physical guidance

2   Locates own timetable and resources

3   Can work from left to right

4   Places finished tasks in designated areas

5   Places resources in the correct place

6   Can move to next activity based on following timetable

7   Tidies up own resources after an activity

8   Checks timetable independently

9   Can use play and leisure time productively

10 Can collect own resources for activities (eg pencil)

11 Can identify resources necessary for tasks (eg scissors)

12 Organises own resources on arrival at school

13 Organises own resources on departure from school

Skills for learning

1   Able to move through a sequence of adult directed activities

2   Willingly attends one-to-one sessions

3   Remains at one-to-one sessions

4   Willingly attends group sessions

5   Completes tasks

6   Understands cause and effect – objects

7   Stays with group when required

8   Uses information from the environment (eg labels)

9   Can demonstrate 'good listening' (look, sit still, think about words)

10 Can request help

11 Able to follow visual instructions

12 Able to complete picture sequences

13 Remembers verbal instructions

14 Arrives at a designated place in a timely manner

15 Asks for directions if unsure

16 Walks away from an aggressive or dangerous situation

17 Accepts decisions of authority

18 Understands cause and effect – people

19 Understands concepts of 'if' and 'then'

20 Gain an adult's attention appropriately

21 Gain a peer's attention appropriately

22 Uses calming strategies if anxious or angry

23 Reads instructions carefully

24 Follows written instructions

25 Applies previous experience to new situations

26 Seeks additional information to support understanding

27 Can use salient information, eg in literacy comprehension

28 Tolerates interruptions

29 Accepts new requests

30 Understands need for some exceptions to rules

31 Can summarise information

32 Can generalise some learning without instruction

33 Check own work for errors and give and receive compliments

34 Able to try more complex tasks with minimal frustration

35 Evaluates decisions

36 Can say no to peers if there is an activity they don't want to do

37 Can accept a difference of opinion

38 Gives constructive criticism

39 Receives constructive criticism

40 Able to plan a task

Appendix 5: IEP target bank

Learning	
Describe issue	**Target**
	> **To stay on task for _____ minutes**
	> **To ask for help when appropriate**
	> **To follow adult advice when help has been sought**
	> **To try more complex tasks with minimal frustration**
	> **To stay on topic throughout a given task**
	> **To fill in lesson note sheet when information is given**
	> **To fill in note taking sheet when reading text**
	> **To plan a piece of work or project before starting**
	> **To complete task within time set**
	> **To seek additional information to support understanding**
	> **To follow _____ consecutive verbal instructions**
	> **To read and follow written instructions**
	> **To use salient information eg in literacy comprehension**
	> **To summarise information**
	> **To complete tasks in the requested format**
	> **To generalise some learning without instruction**
	> **To read work through when finished and correct some mistakes**
	> **To only use or get ready necessary equipment**
	> **To evaluate decisions**
	> **To tolerate interruptions**
	> **To accept a difference of opinion**
	> **To give constructive criticism**
	> **To receive constructive criticism**

Appendices

Independent work

Describe issue	Target
	> To try a given task before asking for help > To move on to next task or question without prompting > To arrive on time for _____ lessons > To follow resource timetable and bring necessary equipment > To read through written instructions before beginning an independent task > To work independently for _____ minutes > To work independently in own work area > To work without interfering with others > To check own work for errors > To locate own timetable or resource > To organise own resources on arrival at school > To organise own resources on departure from school > To collect own resources for activities (eg pencil) > To tidy up own resources after an activity > To place finished tasks in designated areas > To move between activities without physical guidance > To check timetable independently > To move to next activity based on following timetable

Homework

Describe issue	Target
	> To fill in homework diary > To refer to homework diary and follow it > To try all tasks listed in homework diary > To ask for help with homework when appropriate > To seek advice on homework before it is due to be handed in > To refer to correct page or textbook > To stay on topic when writing assignments > To follow required procedure > To use correct equipment > To hand homework in on time > To complete tasks in the right book > To remember to bring completed homework in > To read comments on homework > To ask if unsure about comments regarding homework > To complete required amount of homework

Working with others

Describe issue	Target
	> To share resources
	> To choose people to interact with
	> To maintain appropriate proximity towards others
	> To use personal contact appropriately
	> To interpret personal contact appropriately
	> To show interest in others' actions or behaviours
	> To take turns in conversations
	> To work with others and not interfere with their property
	> To respond positively when a pupil asks not to talk about a particular subject
	> To stay on topic within a conversation
	> To initiate a conversation appropriately
	> To hold a conversation without becoming offensive
	> To follow 'good listening' with peers
	> To talk at an acceptable speed or volume
	> To close a conversation politely
	> To compromise with peers
	> To partially participate in small groups
	> To fully participate in small groups
	> To partially participate in large groups
	> To fully participate in large groups
	> To partially participate in whole school activities
	> To fully participate in whole school activities
	> To follow explicit group rules
	> To follow implicit group rules
	> To terminate interaction appropriately
	> To tolerate others joining or leaving group
	> To understand impact of own actions on others
	> To make an accurate assumption about others' actions
	> To be aware of explicit social conventions
	> To be aware of implicit social conventions

Appendices

Behaviour during break or transition times

Describe issue	Target
	> To stay in the appropriate area > To leave rooms quietly > To listen to (all) adults > To tidy resources at the end of lesson > To keep personal possessions with you during break or transition times > To go calmly to next lesson when required > To wait when required > To use money appropriately at lunchtimes > To remain on the premises > To have good manners when eating > To join in with others without aggression > To seek out friends at break times > To report necessary cases of bullying or aggression to an adult > To report incidents without retaliating > To travel with visual prompts between areas of school > To travel independently between areas of school

Adhering to school rules on social conduct

Describe issue	Target
	> To apply school rules in all areas of building > To follow the rule for .... > To follow safety rules for .... > To use equipment safely > To be polite during .... > To not hurt others > To not say unkind things to others > To wear school uniform correctly > To follow rules during off-site visits > To stay with class or adult during off-site visits > To walk around school without damaging property > To arrive at and leave school in a calm manner > To follow rules for travelling to and from school > To accept authority figures and speak to them respectfully > To listen to advice from staff without hostility or aggression

Behaviour in class

Describe issue	Target

	> To sit in own seat or area at the start of the day
	> To follow 'good listening'
	> To answer the register appropriately
	> To ask a question appropriately
	> To answer questions appropriately
	> To sit properly at a table
	> To follow expected class routines
	> To begin work without complaining
	> To accept adult direction
	> To accept adult support
	> To sit in a group when required
	> To move around the classroom in a quiet fashion
	> To work in class without distracting others
	> To demonstrate 'active listening' (sitting or standing still, looking at speaker, thinking about words, asking if unsure)
	> To look at another adult or students when spoken directly to
	> To take turns in a conversation
	> To calmly ask for help then wait for a response
	> To follow points to a class discussion
	> To use academic terms like 'discuss', 'contrast' etc.
	> To understand academic terms like 'discuss', 'contrast' etc.
	> To contribute relevant answers or points to a class discussion
	> To understand:
	  > humour
	  > sarcasm
	  > figurative speech
	  > idioms
	  > inference
	  > deduction

Appendices

Self-help and organisational skills

Describe issue	Target
	> To refer to map of school if lost > To request directions > To bring correct resources and equipment to school > To hand in homework on time without reminders > To arrive at the correct lesson on time > To be in correct part of school without reminders > To decide on own lunch > To get or eat own lunch without supervision > To wear correct school uniform > To follow school routines independently > To take own notes for a lesson > To fill in homework diary correctly > To follow own timetable > To use help card when in difficulty > To use safe haven without being requested > To identify when angry or upset > To take an acceptable form of action when angry or upset > To request help if needed > To explain and/or demonstrate problem > To find alternative solutions > To request a demonstration > To request information

Additional issues and targets

Describe issue	Target
	> > > > > > > > > > > >

Appendix 6: symbols

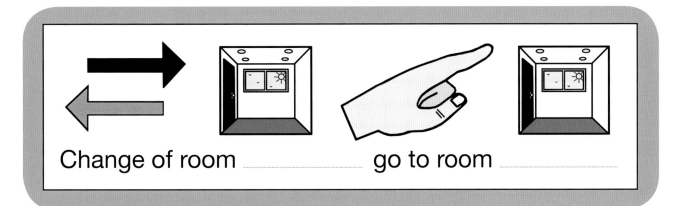

Change of room ———— go to room ————

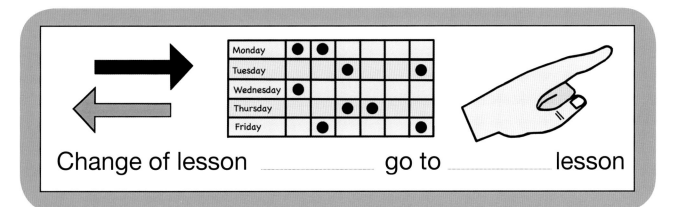

Change of lesson ———— go to ———— lesson

Change of teacher

Appendix 7: symbols to support unstructured times

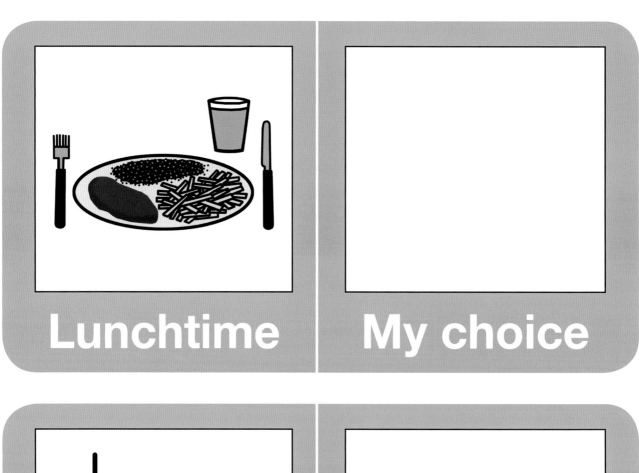

Appendix 8: lesson notes framework

Name:	Lesson notes on (date):
Subject:	Topic:
Key points: **New vocabulary:** **Work to do:** **Resources:** **Questions or clarification:**	

Appendix 9: homework diary

HOMEWORK DIARY	Name:	Day:	Date:		
	Subject and member of staff	Topic	Resources	What to do	Hand in on

Appendix 10: lesson notes framework and prompt list

THINGS TO REMEMBER	
Monday	
Tuesday	
Wednesday	
Thursday	
Friday	

PROMPT LIST		
Textbooks Pens Pencils Notebook Ruler	Games kit Shower gel Towel Ingredients for food tech	Reply slip Money Card or ticket for lunch Library pass Bus pass

Appendix 11: symbols for use in a visual timetable

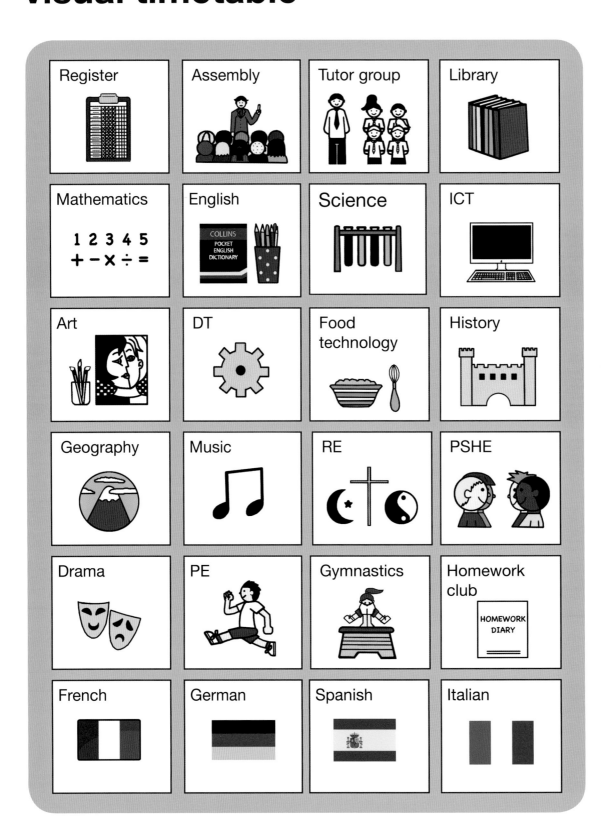

Register	Assembly	Tutor group	Library
Mathematics	English	Science	ICT
Art	DT	Food technology	History
Geography	Music	RE	PSHE
Drama	PE	Gymnastics	Homework club
French	German	Spanish	Italian

Appendix 12: order of tasks

Order of tasks		
1		
2		
3		
4		
5		

Appendix 13: story planner

This style of template can help a pupil construct a story in English or retell an historical event.

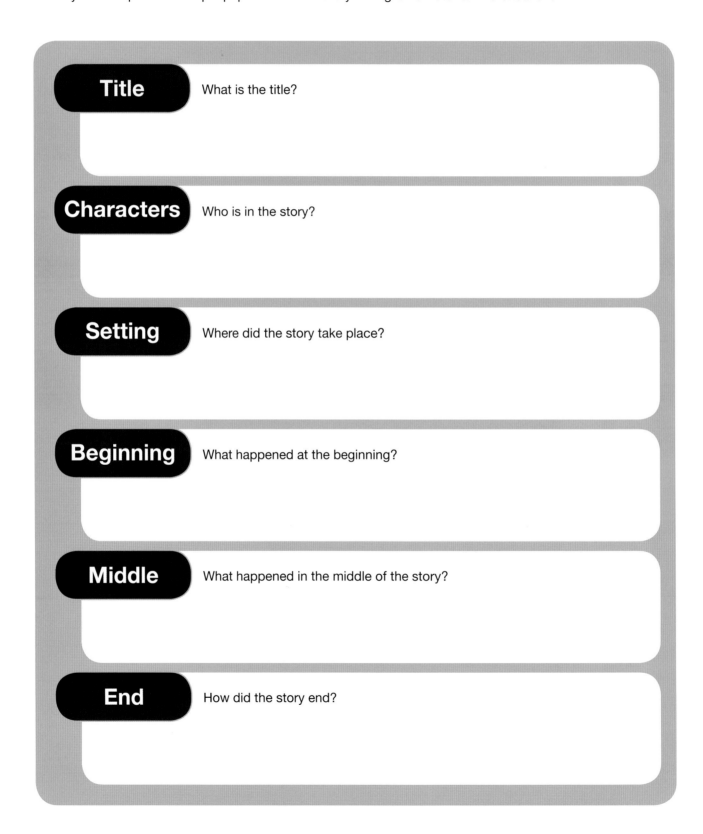

Title — What is the title?

Characters — Who is in the story?

Setting — Where did the story take place?

Beginning — What happened at the beginning?

Middle — What happened in the middle of the story?

End — How did the story end?

Appendix 14: Venn diagram

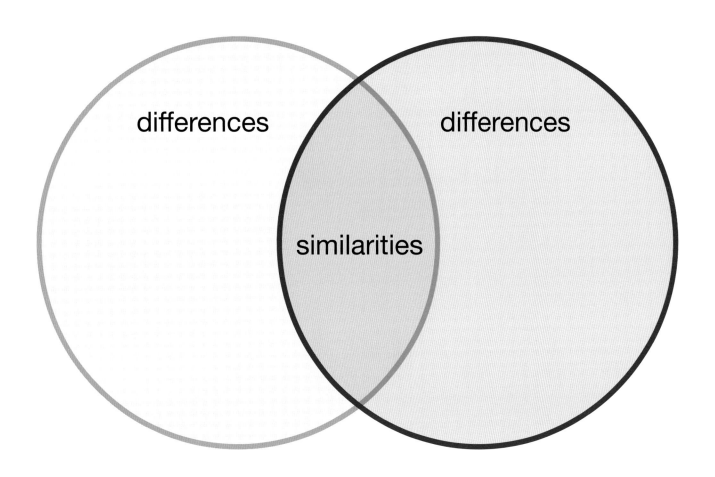

Appendix 15: experiment organiser

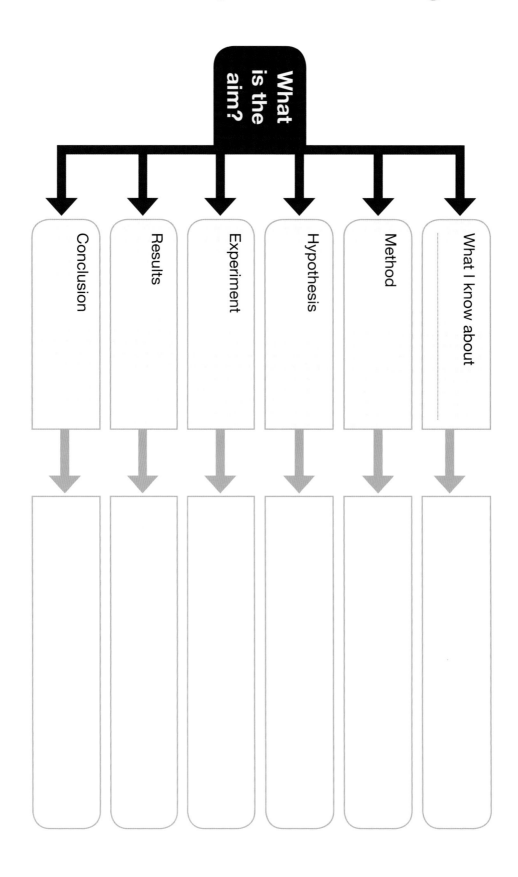

Appendix 16: problem solver

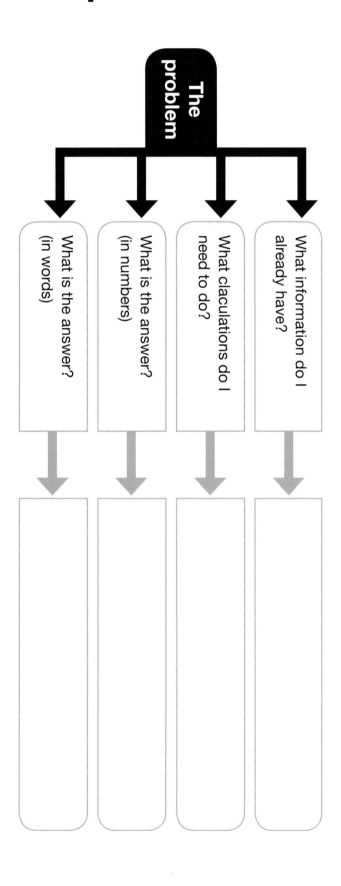

The problem

What is the answer? (in words)

What is the answer? (in numbers)

What claculations do I need to do?

What information do I already have?

Appendix 17: English or history organiser

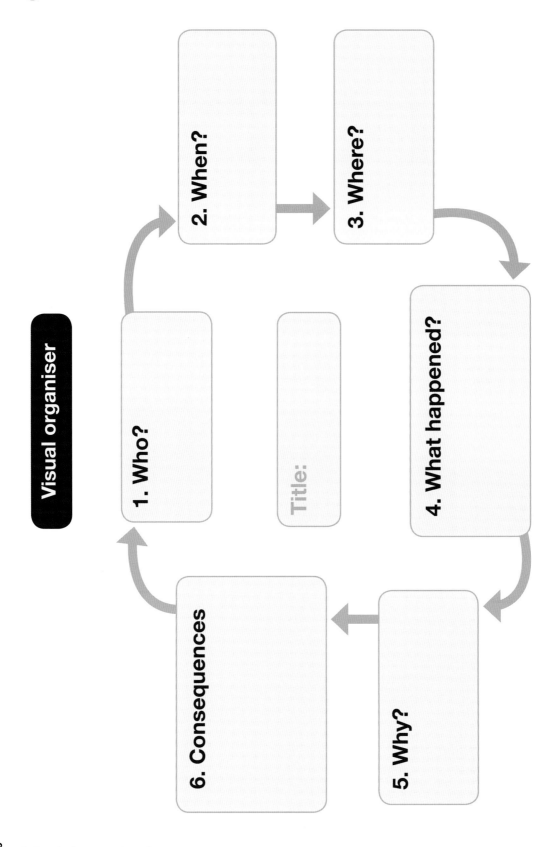

Appendix 18: independent learning organiser

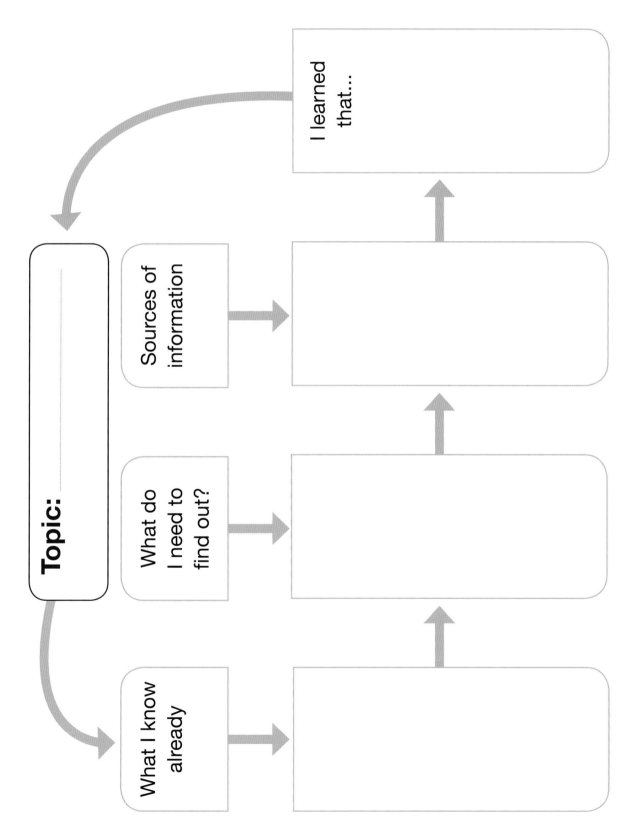

Appendix 19: making a 'balanced decision' template

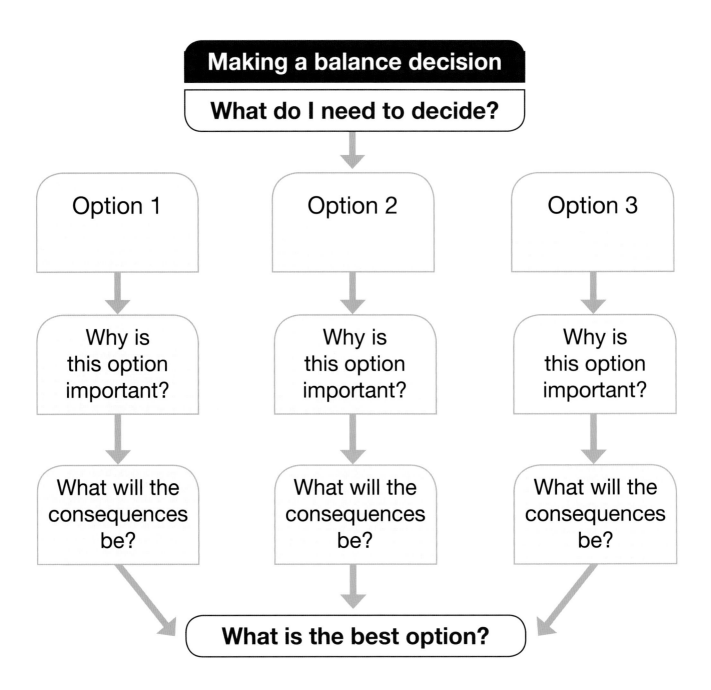

Appendix 20: 'sides of an argument' template

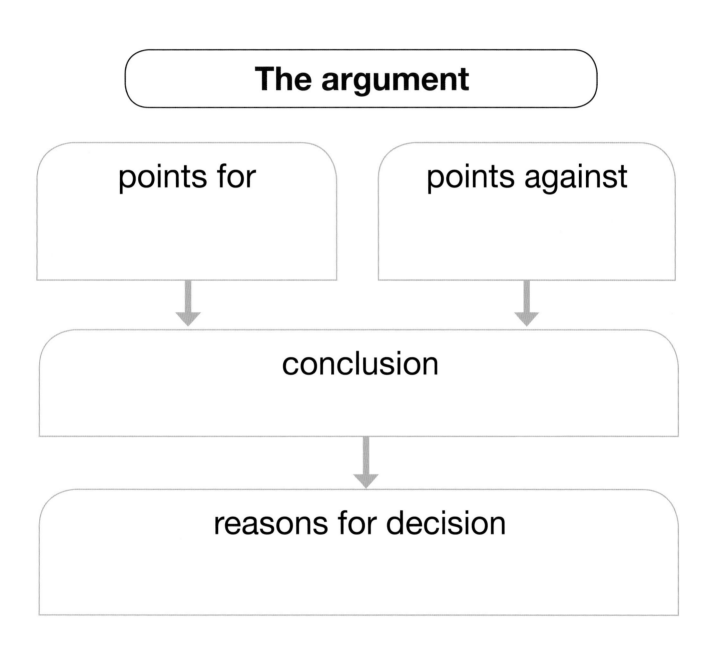

The argument

points for

points against

conclusion

reasons for decision

Appendix 21: observation chart

Observations of behaviour		
Antecendents	**Behaviour**	**Consequences**
Describe what happened before the incident	Describe the incident	Describe what happened after the incident

Appendix 22: angry arrow chart

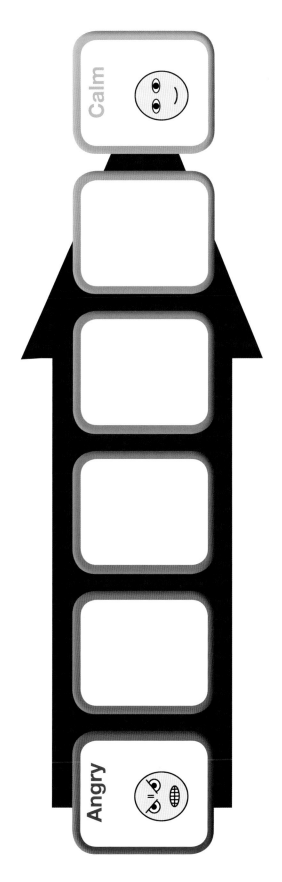

Appendix 23: example of a completed angry arrow chart

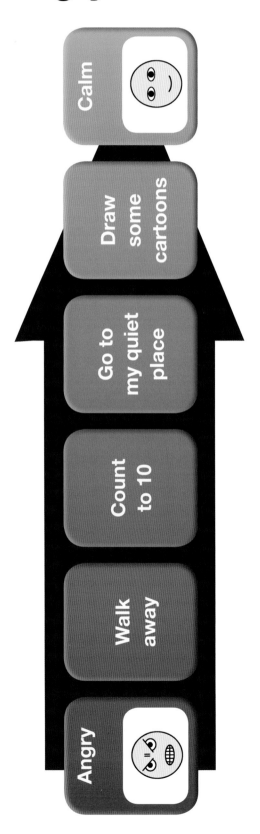

Appendix 24: individual behaviour cards

I have autism.

I may get into a panic.

When I get into a panic I find it difficult to understand speech.

I am very sensitive to sounds.

Please do not touch me.

Please do not stand too close.

Please do not shout.

I have Asperger syndrome.

When I get upset I find it difficult to understand what people want me to do.

Sometimes I do not understand why I have to do things.

I find it helpful when situations are explained to me clearly.

Please talk to me in a quiet voice.

Appendix 25: behaviour chart to develop motivation

_____'s behaviour chart

If I get _____ I can: _____

	Mon	Tues	Weds	Thurs	Fri
🙂					
😐					
🙁					
BREAK					
🙂					
😐					
🙁					
LUNCH					
🙂					
😐					
🙁					

Appendix 26: example of a completed behaviour support plan

Behaviour plans can be used to ensure that all of the staff involved can approach behaviour consistently, and therefore they need to be shared. It may be useful to discuss the behaviour with the student as they may be able to provide some insight into the triggers. Careful consideration should be given to drawing up as many preventative strategies as possible.

Description of behaviour or triggers	Preventative strategies	Early interaction	Adult intervention
____ does not sit down when he enters a classroom but stands in the corner getting more and more agitated	› Ensure that ____ can enter the classroom either first or last › Provide a consistent designated seat that is free from distractions ____ to be shown to seat by an adult or buddy › Notify ____ of arrangements	› Remind ____ of where he (she) sits › Reassure, say "It's OK, this is your seat, please sit down now"	› Direct ____ to his (her) seat › Allow ____ 2–3 minutes to sit down › Give a warning that ____ is expected to sit down › If still not seated, remind ____ that the work will be completed in detention
After lunchtime, ____ does not return to class and has wandered into the kitchen area	› Clearly identify prohibited areas › Remind ____ of importance of timekeeping › Minimise time spent in close proximity to other students when entering building › Use visit to kitchen as a reward › Provide a list of suitable lunchtime activities › Consider use of more secure entry into kitchen	› Staff or 'buddy' to ____ watch › Give warning or countdown towards end of lunchtime › Kitchen staff to remind ____ that he (she) is not allowed inside kitchen	› Return ____ from kitchen area immediately › Highlight the fact that ____ is late for lessons
____ visits office several times per day and demands to know how long there is left to the school day	› Check that ____ can tell the time › Use a social story for school times › Ensure ____ has a personal timetable with timings of the day and locations › After each lesson, remind ____ when school will finish › Remind ____ that office staff should not be disturbed › Provide a list of who to get help from › Incorporate an enjoyable or relaxing activity if ____ finds the day stressful	› Office staff to remind ____ to check his timetable and say "Please do not disturb us we are busy. Look at your timetable" › Adults to direct ____ to next lesson as soon as possible	› Adult to redirect ____ away from the office area › Use a designated place for ____ to calm down if necessary

Appendix 27: blank behaviour support plan

Description of behaviour or triggers	Preventative strategies	Early interaction	Adult intervention

Appendix 28: transition checklist from primary to secondary school

Transition checklist from primary to secondary school

Spring term – student in year six at primary school

1   Liaise with secondary school SENCO.
2   List key dates, available staff meetings, INSET days, suitable dates for visits or meetings etc.
3   Decide on any staff training that may be required.
4   Arrange dates for future visits or meetings.

Summer term: student in year six at primary school

1   Raise awareness for staff.
2   Deliver training packages.
3   Identify key adults and workers.
4   Draw up specific ASD provision with particular student in mind.
5   Discuss transition with the pupil – introduce changes gradually.
6   Give the student details of the school – geographical, numbers of students and classes etc.
7   Primary school SENCO to visit secondary school with ASD pupil.
8   Key adults to meet the pupil.
9   Meeting of adults involved.
10 Prepare information, behaviour plan, Social Story™, etc.
11 Display maps, labels and visuals in school, ready for September.
12 Student to meet adults again and some secondary students.
13 Give out map of building and any other essential details of school.
14 Arrange taster day(s).
15 Prepare behaviour plans, Social Stories™, information sheet, ready for September.

Autumn term: student begins at secondary school

1   Have routines, behaviour plans and timetable ready for first day.
2   Introduce student to new routines, eg what happens at lunchtime; use Social Story™ if applicable.
3   Ensure all adults have met the student and have copies of relevant information.
4   Identify a 'safe haven' for the student to go to during particularly difficult times.
5   Decide with the student seating arrangements for each lesson.
6   Identify suitable students for group work for each lesson.
7   Raise awareness among other students, if appropriate.
8   Introduce learning strategies that will enable the student to take notes, complete homework, organise resources and cope with demanding situations.

Appendix 29: transition checklist from school or college to work

Transition checklist from school or college to work

Identifying suitable careers

1 Liaise with careers guidance officer if there is one in your school or college.
2 List possible careers.
3 Ask your careers adviser if there is a skills audit available or an electronic job database that can be accessed.
4 List strengths, interests and challenges.
5 Research some of the possible jobs on the internet, drawing attention to any areas that the students may find especially easy or difficult.
6 Check through job advertisements so the student understands the availability of different job opportunities.
7 Remember that most jobs have a social element to them, so refer to social skills and the level of social expectations explicitly.
8 Identify two or three suitable jobs.
9 Be clear about the nature and length of any additional qualifications that may be required.
10 Contact potential local employers to arrange visits.

Preparation for interviews

1 Students who have identified a specific job advert may need guidance about their suitability for that particular post.
2 Offer to check and/or help with application forms that need to be filled in.
3 Explain that interviews are generally required and what interviews are for.
4 List and practise all aspects of the interview, eg waiting to be interviewed, entering a room, where to sit.
5 If the student finds the initial introductory phase difficult then consider practising an opening script.
6 Write a Social Story™ for job interviews; this could be used with lots of other students.
7 Highlight the relevance and importance of making a good impression.
8 An interview 'do' and 'don't' list may be useful.
9 Explain that all of the questions are specifically related to the job, eg asking about hobbies usually means hobbies that are related to the job applied for.
10 List common interview questions and prepare answers.
11 Practise interviews with familiar adults.
12 Remember that interviews may be particularly stressful for students with autism so it is important to gauge stress levels throughout the interview preparation stage.

Transition checklist from school or college to work

Starting work or work experience

1. Identify types of suitable work and then the specific organisation and workplace.
2. Plan a preparatory visit.
3. Prepare a list of questions with the student to ask during the preparatory visit.
4. Remember to plan travel to and from the workplace if the applicant will need to make the journey independently.
5. Prepare a timetable ready for the first day.
6. Introduce student to new routines, eg lunchtimes, and provide social story if applicable.
7. Ensure all colleagues have met the student and have copies of relevant information.
8. Identify a 'safe haven' for the student to go to during particularly difficult times.
9. Raise awareness among other colleagues, if appropriate.
10. Introduce strategies that will enable the student to:
    > deal with the general public if appropriate
    > remember instructions
    > know how and when to get help
    > organise his or her own belongings
    > cope with demanding situations.

Notes